THE BIG DISCONNECT

THE BIG DISCONNECT

WHY THE INTERNET

HASN'T TRANSFORMED
POLITICS (YET)

MICAH L. SIFRY

OR Books

New York · London

© 2014 Micah L. Sifry
For all rights information: rights@orbooks.com

Published by OR Books, New York and London
Visit our website at www.orbooks.com

First printing 2014

Cataloging-in-Publication data is available from the Library of Congress.
A catalog record for this book is available from the British Library.

ISBN 978-1-939293-50-3 paperback
ISBN 978-1-939293-51-0 e-book

Typeset by Lapiz Digital, Chennai, India.
Printed by BookMobile in the United States and CPI Books Ltd in
the United Kingdom. The U.S. printed edition of this book comes on
Forest Stewardship Council-certified, 30% recycled paper. The printer,
BookMobile, is 100% wind-powered.

TABLE OF CONTENTS

This is a book for social and political activists.

FOREWORD

At the start, I want to define four key terms you will encounter in this book: the Internet, Big Data, Politics, and Democracy.

When I refer to the Internet, I first mean the set of protocols and practices that allow computing and communications devices to connect to each other and share information, and second the set of cultural behaviors and expectations that this underlying foundation makes possible. Those ideas and practices include open source software, open data, interoperability, linking, and transparency, as well as the fundamental freedom to connect.[1] I do not think these are immutable principles that the technology of the network guarantees, but rather these are highly contested and endangered values that all kinds of powerful interests would love to contain or suppress.

The Internet as we have known it from its birth in the late 1960s to the present date is, simultaneously, an act of selfless coordination by many public-spirited engineers, a lucky accident, and a highly efficient way to solve the problem of connecting different computing and communications devices together. It is also in danger of being destroyed by a combination of greed (on the part of big tech companies who are walling it off), laziness (on the part of users who are choosing free and convenient services over a more decentralized and personally secure architecture), and nationalism (on the part of some countries that fear the freedom that the Internet makes possible and on the part of others that are using it maliciously to spy on and attack adversaries). The experience of being able to read, write, and connect freely to anyone else using the Internet is producing a momentous and precious shift in our culture towards greater self-awareness and voice on the part of individuals and groups. This is worth expanding and defending.

Next, what is Big Data? When I use this term, I mean the capacity to collect massive amounts of raw information for later processing at relatively low cost. Until a few years ago, it was quite expensive to amass large amounts of data and analyze it fast enough to derive significant value from it. When the cost of collection, processing, and analysis was prohibitive, people were forced to limit their data gathering. But the speed and capacity of computer chips have doubled every eighteen to twenty-four months, per Moore's Law, driving costs to the floor. That fact, along with the rise of cloud computing and new processing platforms, has made past limits on big data obsolete. We can now observe and record nearly every human and digital interchange, meaning that more institutions (not just the National Security Agency) are collecting as much data as possible. And data analytics, the procedures and tools that we can use to derive meaning from raw data, are the new Holy Grail.

What about Politics? I believe that politics encompasses everything that we can and must do *together*. It includes how we educate our children, design our communities and neighborhoods, feed ourselves and dispose of our wastes, how we care for the sick and elderly and the poor, how we relate to the natural world, how we entertain and enlighten ourselves, how we defend ourselves and what values we seek to defend, what roles are chosen for us by virtue of our identity and what roles we create for ourselves. It is how we sort out, together, what kind of society we want, what kind of country we want, and what kind of world we want. Politics also means being able to ask—ask as a community, not just as individuals isolated from each other—fundamental questions about where we are going and what the future should be for the generations that follow.

Finally, what is Democracy? Democracy is, simply, the system of government by which the people govern themselves. It is an aspiration that no one anywhere has yet achieved. As the Czech playwright Vaclav Havel told the U.S. Congress in February 1990, "As long as people are people, democracy, in the full sense of the word, will always be no more than an ideal. One may approach it as one would the horizon in ways that may be better or worse, but it can never be fully attained."[2] But the goal of democracy is the condition where all people can participate fully and equally in the decisions that affect their lives. That is my lodestar.

Havel's words should haunt us:

> *Interests of all kinds: personal, selfish, state, national, group and, if you like, company interests still considerably outweigh*

genuinely common and global interests. We are still under the sway of the destructive and thoroughly vain belief that man is the pinnacle of creation, and not just a part of it, and that therefore everything is permitted. There are still many who say they are concerned not for themselves but for the cause, while they are demonstrably out for themselves and not for the cause at all. We are still destroying the planet that was entrusted to us, and its environment. We still close our eyes to the growing social, ethnic and cultural conflicts in the world. From time to time we say that the anonymous megamachinery we have created for ourselves no longer serves us but rather has enslaved us, yet we still fail to do anything about it.[3]

Let's do something about it.

—Micah L. Sifry, March 2014

1

The Revolution That Wasn't

*"The Net, the very network itself, you see, is merely a means
to an end. The end is to reverse-engineer government, to
hack Politics down to its component parts and fix it."*
—Joshua Quittner, "The Merry Pranksters Go to
Washington," *Wired Magazine*, June 1994

I love the Internet.
I hate the Internet.

I love the Internet because anybody can connect to it, nobody
owns it, and anyone can improve it.[1] It's the ultimate proof that
organized anarchism is not an oxymoron.

But more importantly, I love the Internet because it makes
it easier to "find the others," as Timothy Leary once said.[2] This
can save lives, foster community, and sometimes make us more
powerful.

When activist and software designer Jim Gilliam was
stricken with his second bout of cancer and needed a double

lung transplant, no hospital would take him. His past battle with lymphoma had left his lungs badly scarred, and he was deemed too high a risk for surgery. He had also previously lost his mother to cancer after growing up as a evangelical Christian; as a result, he had lost his faith in God:

> I was pissed. So I blogged about it. I called the surgeons at UCLA a few names which I probably shouldn't repeat here. But then something amazing happened. One of the volunteers from Brave New Films [the company he worked for at the time] saw my post and wrote an email to the generic UCLA email address accusing them of only doing easy surgeries to inflate their survival rates. Then my sister wrote an email, then all my friends sent emails.

> Two weeks later the scheduler from UCLA called to set up an appointment. I told her they had already rejected me, she said "I don't know, but I've got you on my list, you need an appointment."

> When I met with the surgeon he said he had been forwarded the emails. My case had been rejected before it had even gotten to him. Lung transplant surgeons have many great qualities, but humility is certainly not one of them. No one was going to accuse him of being afraid of anything.

> There were many more hurdles to jump. Normally it takes a couple weeks to get on the list; it took me months. The insurance

companies tried to weasel out of it, the transplant board kept coming up with excuses, more tests were ordered each week. But my family, friends, their friends, and a bunch of people from the Internet fought every step of the way, and I got on the list.

Eventually, he got the lung transplant and is now running a successful political technology start-up called NationBuilder. Gilliam says the Internet is literally his religion. "God is what happens when humanity is connected," he declared at the end of his talk at the Personal Democracy Forum in 2011, an annual conference I run along with Andrew Rasiej.

Since the Internet is making us more connected, Gilliam believes in it. His experience of being supported by hundreds of people through the Internet restored his faith—not in the traditional concept of God, but in humanity.[3]

Sometimes the Internet makes it easier for people with a common story to come together. After a terrible rash of suicides by young gay men in the middle of 2010, writer Dan Savage and his partner Terry Miller made a YouTube video that spoke directly to those kids in trouble. They shared their own experiences of being bullied when they were young, and promised, "It gets better."[4] They didn't know what they were doing; they just followed their hearts. That video started an online movement, as people shared it and started posting their own versions.

Things really took off a few weeks later, when, in Fort Worth, Texas, a city councilman named Joel Burns made an emotional speech during a public hearing, explaining how he had nearly committed suicide as a young gay man, also assuring the world that "it gets better." His testimony was captured by the city council's video camera, and has since been seen nearly three million times on YouTube.[5] With some volunteer help and a website (ItGetsBetter.org), the It Gets Better Project soon became a real organization, generating 50,000 similar videos from groups and individuals (including Major League Baseball teams, President Barack Obama, and Secretary of State Hillary Clinton), and millions of dollars in donations for crisis counseling for gay teens at risk.

Sometimes the Internet is just an invisible safety net. A few years ago, I was stranded in central Europe for several days, after speaking at a conference in Berlin, when ash from a volcanic eruption in Iceland closed airports across the continent. Twitter was my lifeline. I asked my followers for advice on how to get back home: What airports were still open? How should I get to them? Where should I go on my way? Random people and acquaintances, following my plight in real-time, helped me with informed answers. Go south, they said, to southern Italy or Spain, where planes were still flying. I wasn't the only person doing this; the Twitter term "#ashtag" was being widely used by travelers those weeks to share information about conditions across Europe.

I made it to Rome, bought a ticket back home, but then I had two days to kill. Wandering the ancient city, at one point, I stopped to post a picture of a beautiful square to my Twitter feed. A half hour later, walking through a different part of the city, someone called my name. A follower of mine on Twitter had just seen the photo I posted, figured I was nearby, and then recognized me on the street. I was alone, but I never felt alone.

To be connected to others, whether navigating unfamiliar territory or sharing a common interest, is inherently empowering. And as the network spreads, our chances of connecting to the "right" people keep improving. Thanks to the Internet, chance meetings leading to real connections are happening more often. Your serendipitous findability—the odds that you will fortuitously connect with someone you don't know but share an interest with—is going up. Connections sometimes lead to collaboration, and when people do things together, that creates trust and social cohesion. And those things help create people power. Sometimes, when other conditions are also ripe, that web of connections has helped enable mass action capable of challenging entrenched power, even dictatorships. So, when we say that we think the Internet can change the world for the better, it's because of how it enables more vital connections to happen between people with respect to the things that they care about.

All of this makes me love the Internet.

Remember what civic life was like before we had the net? Like-minded people still found each other, but it was harder to do. You had to travel to common gathering places and hope to find the right people, with fewer hints as to who that might be. Or, if you were trying to organize an event, you had to make flyers, print them, stuff them in envelopes, address them, buy and lick the stamps, and trundle everything off to the post office.

It could take hours of work and days of waiting just to reach a hundred people. And if you were in the political news business, as I was, and you were trying to reach a large audience with a dissenting point of view, you had to figure out how to convince one of the handful of gatekeepers—the people who decided what got onto one of the three nightly TV news shows or onto the op-ed pages of one of the four or five influential newspapers—that you deserved a hearing.

For anyone trying to challenge the status quo by getting on the public stage, things were worse a generation ago. They're better now.

But I hate the Internet, too.

Yesterday, I sent 47 emails and received 367 in return. Some days I send more than 100, and receive more than 500. There are more than 73,000 currently in my inbox. Google says I sent 817 and received 7,377 from more than 1,500 people in the last month. No wonder my brain hurts. How about yours?

The average office worker spends nearly 30 percent of her workday handling email.[6] This is a kind of work that didn't even exist a generation ago. And we don't have much choice but to deal with it. A lot of the emails I get are from people I work with. Those definitely demand my attention. A few are from family and friends. I don't want to ignore those either. Some are from listservs that I belong to. Arguably those can be ignored, but good list-servs are valuable tracking tools. They keep me informed and engaged, and often expose me to points of view that I otherwise might not hear.

Some emails can be consumed and responded to in seconds. Others actually contain, compressed within their electronic confines, hours of work, demanding equivalent time and attention in response. They come "overwinded," to use Douglas Rushkoff's phrase. "The problem is that the sender may have spring-loaded a whole lot of time and energy into that message so that clicking on it is like opening a Pandora's box of data and responsibilities," he writes in his recent book *Present Shock.* "A week of the sender's preparation can instantaneously flow into our present."[7]

Temporal compression isn't new. Humans have been binding time into tighter packages for ages, Rushkoff notes. Civilization and culture are the knowledge and experiences of many generations compressed into digestible and learnable forms. But now, with so much knowledge available, so many opportunities for self-expression, so many experiences being shared, and so many demands on our attention, our experience of time itself, Rushkoff argues, is being radically transformed.

The future is here and it's breaking the present, with damaging effects on both our personal lives as well as our collective awareness.

Rushkoff was once a digital utopian:

> *Along with most technology hopefuls of the twentieth century, I was one of the many pushing for more connectivity and openness as the millennium approached. It seemed the only answer for our collapsing, top-down society was for everyone*

and everything to network together and communicate better and more honestly . . . a connected world would respond more rapidly and emphatically to crises in remote regions, it would become more aware of threats to its well-being, and may actually become more cooperative as a whole.[8]

But being hyper-networked has not only hyper-empowered small groups to the point where they can destabilize nation-states (see, for example, Al Qaeda or Wall Street derivatives traders), it is also challenging how we move through daily life.

"We can produce effects in more than one place at a time, each of us now having the global reach formerly reserved for kings, presidents, and movie stars," writes Rushkoff. "Our role in the culture and society may have changed from that of passive readers or watchers to that of active game players, but this self-direction comes at a cost . . . we must keep our eyes moving at the same time to stay aware of all sorts of activity on the periphery."[9]

And that means managing multiple digital presences far more complicated than email alone—dividing our attention even further. Take Twitter. If I leave a tab open just to watch tweets flow in as I write these words, in five minutes I've got 66 new ones to read, because I follow about 3,000 people. At that rate, I'll have nearly 20,000 new tweets to read each day. Obviously I'm not going to read them all. I long ago learned to watch Twitter for the overall flow. For instance, tools like TweetedTimes.com, which aggregate the top links from people I follow, may give me 20–30 top headlines to peruse. But this also takes time.

I tend to pay attention to people active in the worlds of politics and technology, and interestingly enough, the politerati and technorati aren't all that different. We mostly do three things on Twitter: we promote ourselves and our work; we respond to a wide variety of current events; and we chat or argue with each other. Occasionally we all pay attention to the same thing at the same time—usually a major live event in politics, sports, or entertainment. Most of the things we tweet about are quickly forgotten. I remember when Twitter was a cure for boredom; now sometimes boredom seems like a cure for Twitter.

As I write this, I've got 27 tabs open on my browser. Some point to long articles that I'm looking forward to reading; others lead to unfinished Google docs that I'm in the process of editing. My web browser, like my email inbox, is overwound with compressed information, some of it representing deferred pleasure and some of representing deferred labor. Between new emails, new tweets, and open tabs, every day my laptop can hypothetically generate enough demands to consume a whole day.

This isn't just a personal problem. These increasing demands on our individual attention—and the fragmentation of concentration that results—are also reflected at the societal level. The future isn't only breaking the present, it's also degrading our ability to move forward as a society.

I first noticed this about five years ago, when for two whole weeks Americans were transfixed by the momentous post-election protests in Iran. And then, all of a sudden, Michael Jackson died, causing the nation's attention to immediately turn elsewhere. The King of Pop's passing held us in thrall, right up until Sarah Palin resigned her governorship of Alaska. Then the Senate confirmed Sonia Sotomayor's nomination to the Supreme Court. Then Senator Ted Kennedy died. Then Nidal Hasan shot up the Fort Hood army base. Then Obama announced the Afghanistan troop surge. Then a Nigerian man tried to blow up a flight from Amsterdam to Detroit on Christmas Day with a bomb in his underwear. Then Haiti was hit with a horrific earthquake. Then Scott Brown took Ted Kennedy's seat. Then there was the Winter Olympics, the earthquake in Chile, the passage of health care reform, the Iceland volcano, and the BP oil spill . . .

Remember not long ago, when America was focused on gun control after the horrific massacre at Sandy Hook Elementary School? Or how we were finally talking about dealing with climate change after Hurricane Sandy? Or how both parties finally seemed ready to compromise on comprehensive immigration reform? To be sure, there are other reasons politics in America is so gridlocked and frustrating. But our attention is undisputedly fragmented by our increasing immersion in all forms of media.

Figure 1, located on page 234, was made by Suman Deb Roy and provided to me by his colleague, Gilad Lotan, the chief data scientist at BetaWorks, a New York City–based venture capital firm that invests in network-focused media companies. According to Lotan, the chart

highlights volatility of Twitter's trending topics for some U.S. cities between January and April 2012. The higher the line on the y-axis, the more topics appeared within Twitter's trend-ing topics that day for the given city. The more topics trending in a day, the less focus or attention given to a single issue or topic. Alternatively, the lower a point is on the plot, the more focused a city is in terms of topics that are trending.[10]

Twitter doesn't disclose the details of the algorithm it uses to determine whether a topic is "trending," but it does say that it is designed to "identif[y] topics that are immediately popular, rather than topics that have been popular for a while."[11] The cities covered include New York City, Los Angeles, Chicago, Houston, Seattle, Austin, Baton Rouge, and Boston, so we're looking at the behavior of a broad swath of American Twitter users with this data set.

As you can see, there is only one day in the four-month period when the attention of those cities' Twitter users was focused on fewer than one hundred topics; most days the number of trend-ing topics fluctuates between 500 and 1000.

The anomalous day is March 8, 2012, three days after the posting of a 30-minute YouTube video by the organization Invisible Children called "KONY 2012."[12] The unusual video tells the story of Invisible Children's passionate effort to end the recruitment of child soldiers in Africa by bringing one warlord, Joseph Kony, to justice. Though flawed in many ways, the video packs an emotional wallop. After being retweeted by a number of Hollywood celebrities, "KONY 2012" went viral faster than any-thing ever before.

By March 8, it had been viewed more than 35 million times on YouTube, a record at the time. (Ultimately more than 100 million watched it.) Young people in particular were spreading it through their online networks faster than the mainstream media. A top State Department official said he first heard about it because his thirteen-year-old daughter brought it to his attention. She had seen it online before him.[13] When one of President Obama's national security advisers tried to tell him about it, he reportedly said, "I know all about that. Malia [his fourteen-year-old daughter] talked about it over dinner last night."[14]

The KONY 2012 video made a huge splash. The immediate clamor of public concern that it created was so great that the U.S. Senate passed a resolution calling for Kony's capture. But the video itself turned out to be the anti-Kony movement's high point. Its very popularity spurred a smaller, but influential, wave of intense criticism from experts who questioned its geopolitical claims and from Africans who said its message was flawed because it reinforced the "white-savior industrial complex."[15] Days after it appeared, the founder of Invisible Children, who was featured in the video, suffered a public nervous breakdown, which he later blamed in part on the media overload.[16]

Even more confounding: the KONY 2012 video also included a call to action, which was intended to make Kony's name so notorious that he would be arrested by the end of 2012. Volunteers were asked to join a "Cover the Night" effort on April 20 to paper cities all over the world with posters demanding his arrest. But six weeks later, few people actually took part. Their attention had drifted elsewhere.[17]

What are we to make of the KONY 2012 movement's explosive growth and subsequent decline? Some of my friends in the world of online organizing thought the video represented the future of digitally-driven messaging.[18] To them, the only mistake that Invisible Children made was that it wasn't ready with enough experienced organizers to channel their sudden attention in more strategic ways. In their opinion, savvy online politicking means understanding how to convert moments into movements.

However, I think they're chasing a mirage, and the tools they are relying on for the chase are pushing the oasis of meaningful political engagement further out of reach. Not that long ago, I thought that the spectacle-and-crisis-driven news cycle offered an opportunity to would-be do-gooders. "Are you ready for the next big disaster?" I asked my activist friends. "Because you will be deluged by volunteers calling you and emailing you offering help; are you ready to channel all that distributed power?"

Huge disasters keep occurring and some volunteers do show up to help. The Internet does often lead some people to say, "Let's get together and do something to fix this." However, I've started to wonder if the bigger trend is atomization; a combination of "let's watch it by ourselves" and "let's respond to it by ourselves." In the case of KONY 2012, millions of people were temporarily transfixed by a powerful piece of propaganda rather than a natural disaster, but that burst of concentrated attention also failed to get most to do anything.

These days, when news happens, the media (old and new) tries to capture our attention with the spectacle, the better to sell ads while we're watching their channel or visiting their website. If the news is powerful enough, we'll consume it together, but we're still just watching, not participating in making it. At the same time, all kinds of social and political actors bombard us with urgent messages, the better to convert our concern into donations or email sign-ups or a click on a "share this" button. Politicians or organizers rarely try to convert attention into more complex forms of engagement and commitment. And when they do, they're fighting powerful crosscurrents, because the media (and many of their peers in politics and advocacy) will soon jump to the next distracting spectacle.

The Internet has made it easier to find the others, but *it is also making it harder to bind with each other with common focus.* We collectively send out far more noise than signal, and we listen far less than we talk. We may not like to admit it, but our digital tools are shaping us far more than we are using them to reshape the world. We need better tools, a challenge that I will cover later in this book.

A decade ago, many of us thought that the rise of open, networked communication was going to move the political needle in a better direction, towards a society where more people had an effective voice and could participate in the decisions that affected their own lives, and towards a government that was more open, participatory, and accountable.

Here's how political strategist Joe Trippi, who managed Howard Dean's 2004 campaign for president, imagined it would happen, in his book *The Revolution Will Not Be Televised—Democracy, The Internet, and the Overthrow of Everything*:

> *One day in the very near future we'd build huge, involved communities around political issues and candidates . . . these people would be an army, ready to mobilize at the first sign that the government was doing that top-down, trust-us-we-know-what's-best-for-you crap that people were so sick of. Government, the entertainment industry and corporate America better get ready. The American people are going to learn how to organize themselves and then watch out.[19]*

Meetup's founder Scott Heiferman mused about the "Napsterization of organization," imagining that in the same way Napster had turned every kid with a computer into a music sharer, the Internet was about to generate a flowering of distributed democracy: "We're in the emergent organization business," he said at a December 2004 conference on "Votes, Bits and Bytes" that the Berkman Center for Internet & Society held at Harvard Law School. "From flash mobs and brick associations to flash, emergent, people-powered long-lasting open, influential, agile, chapter-based institutions and organizations that have card-carrying members," he declared, "Net-based collective action and group power has hardly begun."[20]

And here's how Eli Pariser and Justin Ruben, the youthful leaders of MoveOn.org's political action committee, saw things after the 2004 election—the first election where grassroots Internet activism achieved a national scale:

> *For years, the [Democratic] party has been led by elite Washington insiders who are closer to corporate lobbyists than they are to the Democratic base. But we can't afford four more years of leadership by a consulting class of professional election losers. . . . In the last year, grass-roots contributors like us gave more than $300 million to the Kerry campaign and the DNC [Democratic National Committee], and proved that the party doesn't need corporate cash to be competitive. Now it's our party: we bought it, we own it, and we're going to take it back.[21]*

It wasn't just people on the left who thought Internet-powered movements were going to democratize politics. In 2005, conservative talk-radio host Hugh Hewitt was so sure that blogging was in the process of undermining liberal media that he wrote a whole book about it called *Blog: Understanding the Information Reformation That's Changing Your World*. Hewitt argued that mainstream figures such as Senator Trent Lott, Democratic presidential candidate John Kerry, CBS anchor Dan Rather, and *The New York Times* editor Howell Raines had been undone by persistent criticism and muckraking led mainly by conservative bloggers (and some helpful liberals). He believed that the right could permanently enshrine this political advantage if it understood where technology was taking America:

> *Now anyone with an internet connection and some basic skills can join the fray. The talented ones gain readers and, with readers, influence. The smart bloggers who have been at it for a few years do what they can to promote the good, young talent. A decade from now the bloggers who dominate today's traffic monitoring sites will almost all have declined or ceased to exist. New voices will have arisen. If the center Right puts a production system into place now and nurtures it with encouragement and attention, it will have the infrastructure to continue to dominate the information dissemination phase of campaigning. High consumers of information are always going to be out there prowling for data and opinions. The party that organizes to meet that demand wins in the long run.*[22]

Back in 2004, it seemed as though we were on the cusp of a major shift in America's civic life. "New tools and practices born on the Internet have reached critical mass, enabling ordinary people to participate in processes that used to be closed to them," I wrote in an essay for *The Nation*, which appeared a week after the re-election of President George W. Bush to his second term:

> *It may seem like cold comfort for Kerry supporters now, but the truth is that voters don't have to rely on elected or self-appointed*

leaders to chart the way forward anymore. The era of top-down politics—where campaigns, institutions and journalism were cloistered communities powered by hard-to-amass capital—is over. Something wilder, more engaging and infinitely more satisfying to individual participants is arising alongside the old order....

New web-based tools are facilitating a different way of doing politics, one in which we may all actually, not hypothetically, be equals; where transparency and accountability are more than slogans; and where anyone with few resources but a compelling message can be a community organizer, an ad-maker, a reporter, a publisher, a theorist, a money-raiser or a leader.

Back then, it seemed as if change was really coming. Lowly political bloggers, laughed at by media big shots for writing in their pajamas from their parents' basements, ignited major media firestorms that humbled national figures. The Talking Points Memo blog, founded by Joshua Micah Marshall (a writer who quit *The American Prospect*, which was still a traditional print magazine), coordinated a massive campaign by volunteers all over the country to get advertisers to boycott Sinclair Broadcasting for planning to run an anti-Kerry documentary just before the election. The campaign was so effective that Sinclair's stock price tanked until the company changed its mind.

And new voices were popping up all the time. A college student working from his dorm room named James Kotecki, who had an amusingly savvy way of reviewing political campaign videos, became a star on YouTube. A Twitter user in London named Amanda Ross rallied her friends in order to launch a grassroots fundraising campaign, the "Twestival," that raised a quarter-million dollars in a few weeks via homegrown events in two hundred cities. A campus activist named Farouk Olu Aregbe created a Facebook group that eventually grew to a million members supporting a presidential candidate, Barack Obama.

We were all optimistic for two reasons. First, the "barrier to entry" into the public conversation was disappearing. The Internet is, by definition, a set of protocols that allow any computer to connect to the larger network. There's no need to get permission from anyone. The inventors of Google didn't need to ask AT&T if it was OK to hook up their nascent search engine to the Internet; they just did it. Nor did the inventors of publishing tools like Blogger, Wordpress, or Movable Type have to seek approval.

And second, the rapid decline in the cost of communicating and connecting was enabling the rise of a "networked public sphere," far different from the older media system built around expensive mass communications systems like television, radio, and newspapers. Millions of new participants in the public conversation were in the process of wresting power away from the old gatekeepers in politics and the press, liberated from the economics of scarce media.

Here's how Harvard Law School professor Yochai Benkler, the author of the term "networked public sphere," imagined that this shift might look (the images are from his 2008 talk at Personal Democracy Forum in New York City):

THE MASS MEDIATED PUBLIC SPHERE

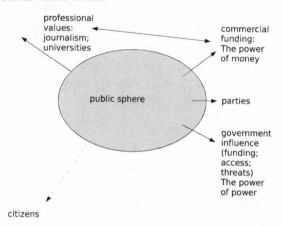

professional values: journalism; universities

commercial funding: The power of money

public sphere

parties

government influence (funding; access; threats) The power of power

citizens

In the mass mediated public sphere, politics is dominated by money, party elites, and government power. Other values that might influence public debate, such as professional or journalistic ethics, or the demands of ordinary citizens, are subordinate to those forces. And for good reason: in a mass mediated public sphere, it's expensive to be heard. Benkler estimates that while it cost James Gordon Bennett $500 to start the *New York Herald* in 1835, by 1850 the entry cost for starting a city newspaper had jumped to $100,000[23] (adjusting for inflation to 2005 dollars, that would be the equivalent of going from $10,000 to

$2.5 million). Publishing went from being something an individual could do to an industrial business enterprise. Commercial values inevitably came to dominate public life, because the media that created public life required a lot of capital. However, in the networked public sphere, the declining cost of communications coupled with mass connectivity shifts the balance of power away from money and centralized institutions and toward citizens and non-market values.

THE NETWORKED PUBLIC SPHERE

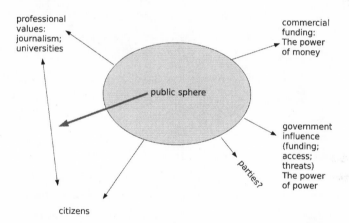

This shift is due to the fact that nearly all of us walk around with a printing press in our pockets that is connected, hypothetically at least, to everyone else. As Benkler writes in his seminal book, *The Wealth of Networks*, "The networked public sphere enables many more individuals to communicate their observations and their viewpoints to many others, and to do so in a way that cannot be controlled by media owners and is not as easily corruptible by money as were the mass media."[24]

Benkler was writing in 2006, when the Internet was just starting to become a mass medium, and scholars and other observers were watching its early effects and debating its impact on society. But critics were already raising important questions about the new media environment. The fear was that the lower cost of communication would lead to information overload, and that as a result, money would still be a critical factor in gaining attention. People also worried that public attention would fragment, and instead of a common public sphere, we'd construct our own "Daily Me," tuning out different viewpoints. Some also fretted that this balkanization would lead to a greater polarization of public life. In the same way that a few publishers or personalities dominated mass media, attention in the networked public sphere would similarly coalesce around a few highly popular sites or speakers.

Benkler offers nuanced responses to each of these criticisms. "Is the Internet in fact too chaotic or too concentrated to yield a more attractive democratic discourse than the mass media did?" he asks. "The observed use of the network exhibits an order that is not too concentrated and not too chaotic, but rather, if not 'just right,' at least structures a networked public sphere more attractive than the mass-media-dominated public sphere."[25]

Information overload is not a serious problem, he argues, because most users solve it "by congregating at a small number of sites."[26] He is not troubled by this development, asserting that while it may be an inevitable consequence of human nature, it does not signal a return to the old days of mass-media. "Indeed, few are read by many," he writes, "but clusters of moderately read sites provide platforms for vastly greater numbers of speakers than were heard in the mass-media environment."[27] In other words, in the new media environment a much larger number of voices are at least partially heard, and if what they have to say is salient, the networked public sphere will propel their content upward towards mass attention.

Benkler cites two political episodes to illustrate this phenomenon: the 2004 boycott of Sinclair Broadcasting, noted above, and the exposure of proprietary documents from Diebold Inc. that showed the company's voting machines could be hacked. In both cases, obscure actors were able to gain rapid and powerful attention by virtue of placing their material online, and powerful corporations were humbled. More recently, Benkler has done equally compelling analyses of the role of WikiLeaks as a watchdog of last resort, and of the unexpected success of the online movement against the Stop Online Privacy Act (SOPA) and the Protect IP Act (PIPA).[28] [29] The latter movement started with just a few small participants and ultimately spread to an Internet-wide blackout by sites like Wikipedia and Google driving millions of emails and phone calls to Congress in January 2012.

In sum, Benkler's case for the democratizing benefits of the new media comes down to this: "The networked public sphere allows hundreds of millions of people to publish whatever and whenever they please without disintegrating into an unusable cacophony . . . and it filters and focuses attention without recreating the highly concentrated model of the mass media. . . ."[30] While there is enormous diversity on the Internet, there are also mechanisms and practices that generate a common set of themes, concerns and public knowledge around which a public sphere can emerge."[31] As for increased polarization, Benkler admits that in the United States, the networked public sphere appears to have congealed into two distinct spheres, one liberal and one conservative, but he argues that there is much cross-linking and commenting between the two sides.

Benkler is right that the new Internet-powered media environment is preferable to the old mass media system. But only up to a point. The networked public sphere does not exist in a vacuum. Its dynamics are also shaped by the tools that we use to traverse it. And joining the public conversation is only one component of exercising power. Indeed, and this is a central point of this book, while the barrier to entry to public media has been lowered by the Internet, the proliferation of digital tools and behaviors has not made participation in decision-making or group coordination substantially easier. With so many more of us creating and sharing content, it may actually be getting harder to reach consensus about common goals.

Worse yet, the primary tool we use—email—has its own inner logic that makes it useful only for certain kinds of coordination, ones that tend to concentrate power in the hands of "Big

Data" collectors and "Big Email" managers. The wonder of email is that it costs (almost) nothing to make more of it. For one-on-one conversations, it works beautifully. But as soon as the list of recipients increases to more than one person, the opportunities for misunderstanding multiply. All un-moderated email lists inevitably result in "flame wars" where, lacking the normal visual cues that might temper emotional responses and dampen disagreement, some people end up viciously attacking each other. Even moderated lists often turn ugly. As a result, the best use of email is to be the owner of a big list where you are writing directly to many atomized individuals who can't respond or talk to each other, but where some fraction will click on a request you make, such as to sign a petition or make a donation.

It is not a coincidence, I think, that all of Benkler's cases of political success—the boycott of Sinclair, the exposure of Diebold, the revelations of WikiLeaks, and the defeat of SOPA/PIPA—are examples of a dispersed network saying "no" to a more concentrated and powerful institution's "yes." That is, each time successful collective action arose because of an external stimulus that propelled sufficient numbers of independent actors to coalesce in opposition—not because those independent actors first brought themselves together in concert.

The Sinclair boycott was a response to the giant media company's outrageous plan to air an anti-Kerry documentary on its news stations just weeks before the 2004 election. The Diebold activists thought they had proof that the company helped steal the 2000 election for Bush, and when its lawyers tried to quash the publication of its internal documents, those activists found many allies willing to risk punishment in exchange for a chance to thumb their nose at a powerful enemy. WikiLeaks benefits from excessive government and corporate secrecy: if such institutions were more open by default, WikiLeaks would get far less attention. In late 2011, when the U.S. government and its officials went after WikiLeaks and got third-parties like Amazon, Visa, PayPal and Mastercard to stop providing WikiLeaks with hosting and commercial services, even people who were unsure whether or not they supported Julian Assange rallied to protect his freedom from organized suppression. Likewise, the scrappy activists who stopped SOPA and PIPA benefited from the fact that the Hollywood interests who drafted those bills were so greedy that they overplayed their own hand.

Occasionally thwarting powerful overlords is not the same thing as transforming the system that confers so many advantages on them into one that is more democratic and effective at representing the interests of all. So far, "the American people" haven't learned how to self-organize, at least not in ways that have radically changed either government or corporate America. That's not to say these things can never happen, just that ten years into the Networked Age they haven't yet, and we need to ask why. The Democratic grassroots didn't take over the Democratic Party; at best they made their champion Howard Dean head of the DNC for a few years, until Barack

Obama won the presidency and took over. Not only have the right's bloggers not taken down many enemies since 2005, but the Republican Party has actually gotten less popular in recent years.

Generally speaking, it's only on the fringes of the political system that we've seen new voices gain new power in America. On the right, libertarian outsider Ron Paul was the first to demonstrate, with his 2008 campaign for president in the Republican primaries, how an Internet-enabled candidate could carve out an independent and viable presence all the way through the national party convention without the support of party leaders or elites. Then in 2010, the Tea Party translated its anti-Obama passion into numerous successful campaigns against moderate Republicans in both the House and Senate. By 2012, the deepest fractures in years were appearing in the Republican Party, as both big money (in the form of newly liberated post-*Citizens United* "SuperPacs" funded by wealthy individuals) and social media networks helped keep several candidates afloat for months, whereas previously the Iowa and New Hampshire primary contests would have given the race to their declared victor, in this case Mitt Romney. The revolt on the Republican right that led to the government shutdown of October 2013 was also powered by a combination of big money and networked grass-roots activism and media.

On the left, the open Internet and connection technologies have given anti-war and pro-civil liberties dissidents like writer Glenn Greenwald a reach that, if we had a multi-party political system, would surely be rewarded with a healthy segment of the popular vote. Some minority voices and causes, particularly those centered on "identity politics," have more salience. And Occupy Wall Street, which was organized almost entirely outside the contours of "normal" American politics by anarchists inspired by the protest movements of Europe and the Arab Spring, was able to briefly upend the political debate and focus attention on inequality in America, a topic that the two major parties uniformly ignore.

But the central contours of American politics really haven't changed all that much in the ten years since the rise of "people-powered" campaigns, or groups like MoveOn, online fundraising hubs like ActBlue, blogs, and social media. The political operating system of big money campaigns, gerrymandered districts, discriminatory ballot access rules which favor the major parties, undisclosed lobbying, and winner-take-all elections hasn't been altered in the slightest.

Consider these facts:

- In 2004, the average cost of winning a seat in the U.S. House of Representatives was $1.26 million (in inflation-adjusted 2012 dollars), according to the Campaign Finance Institute. In 2012 it rose to $1.6 million. On the Senate side, the average winning campaign cost $8.7 million in 2004; in 2012 that average rose to $10.4 million.[32]
- If the Internet was democratizing electoral politics, then

small donors would be stepping up and playing a bigger role in helping candidates clear these tougher thresholds. But on the whole they aren't. In the 2004 cycle, just 8 percent of the money given to House candidates came from donors giving less than $200. In 2012, that percentage inched up to just 10 percent. Big donors (those who give more than $1,000) and PACs still mattered far more to House candidates, delivering a whopping 71 percent of all the money raised in 2012 (which was, in fact, more than in 2004).[33] On the Senate side, the percentage of money going to candidates from donors giving less than $200 didn't change at all: it was 17 percent in 2004 and 17 percent in 2012.[34]

- Political challengers, theoretically the beneficiaries of any surge in participation by small donors, in fact have seen little overall benefit. In the 2004 cycle, House challengers raised 18 percent of their total funds from small donors. In 2012, that percentage dropped to 14 percent. The total amount given by small donors certainly increased, from $16 million to $25 million. But this was dwarfed by an even bigger increase in the role of larger donors. And on the Senate side, while small donations made up a larger percentage of the money flowing to challengers, again there was no real change in the magnitude between 2004, at the dawn of big online fundraising, and in 2012. Senate challengers raised 27 percent of their cash in small donations in 2004, and 26 percent in 2012.[35]

- It's true that the Internet has enabled the rise of a handful of new organizations that bundle contributions to political candidates, especially on the Democratic side of the aisle, and many of these donations are from small donors. In 2012, ActBlue, the biggest online aggregator of Democratic donations, bundled $30 million to House candidates and $18 million to Senate candidates, and slightly more than half of those amounts came from small donors.[36] It's also true that Senator Elizabeth Warren of Massachusetts was able to match Wall Street (which supported her opponent Scott Brown) dollar for dollar with a huge national base of small donors. And self-activating groups of liberal activists working through large community blogs, most importantly DailyKos.com, have sometimes rallied themselves to recruit and raise early money for new candidates, not only in congressional races but sometimes even state legislative fights. But while promising, these are still exceptions to the rule.

- And while technology may be contributing to a modest increase in the number of people making small donations to support candidates or influence the political process, so far this hasn't resulted in a marked change in the class make-up of the political donor pool. According to the 2012 Pew Internet and American Life Survey, analyzed by political scientists Kay Lehman Schlozman, Sidney Verba, and Henry E. Brady, "those who make small donations are relatively unlikely to be drawn from the lower runs of the income ladder. . . . online contributors who donate small amounts are not markedly less affluent than their offline counterparts." They add, "If anything they are actually somewhat better off financially. Thus it seems that the Internet may be bringing in *more* small donors, but it is not bringing in a *less affluent* set of small donors."[37]

- Re-election rates for Congressional incumbents have also barely changed. Yes, in 2010 and 2012 somewhat more incumbents than usual lost their seats in House races—but, respectively, 85 percent and 90 percent were re-elected in those cycles, according to the Center for Responsive Politics. Re-election rates for Senators tend to fluctuate more, since there are fewer races and more competition, but in 2012, 91 percent of sitting Senators up for election were returned to office.[38] The advantages of incumbency (gerrymandered districts, franking privileges, pork, greater media attention) are still quite real.

- Even more shocking, the lowered barrier to entry has not enticed more people to run for state office. In 2012, nearly 40 percent of all state legislative candidates ran for office unopposed by a candidate of the other major party, according to the invaluable Ballot Access News.[39]

And for all the talk of "change you can believe in," and the number of times the media reported that Barack Obama had organized a mass movement using the latest digital technology, and that he would enter office with an army of millions helping him bring real change to Washington, DC, very little changed. Compared to his predecessors, it is true that a much larger base of small donors financed his campaign. But "no part of the system was shaken up," notes David Graeber, one of the early organizers of the Occupy movement, in his recent book, *The Democracy Project*:

> *There were no bank nationalizations, no breakups of 'too big to fail' institutions, no major changes in finance laws, no change in the structure of the auto industry, or of any other industry, no change in labor laws, drug laws, surveillance laws, monetary policy, education policy, transportation policy, energy policy, military policy, or—most crucially of all, despite campaign pledges—the role of money in the political system. In exchange for massive infusions of money from the country's Treasury to rescue them from ruin, industries from finance to manufacturing to health care were required to make only marginal changes to their practices.[40]*

The Internet, and all its attendant forms of connection technology and social media, now permeates the lives of nearly all Americans. In the last fifteen years, being digitally connected has become a nearly universal condition. In 1995, just one in seven American adults were online, according to the Pew Internet & American Life Project. Now more than four out of five are, and among eighteen- to twenty-nine-year-olds the figure is 97 percent. Seventy-three percent of adult Internet users are on social networking sites, whereas just nine years ago that number was 8 percent.[41]

Tens of millions of us are online political activists engaged each day in sifting the news, sharing our concerns, and attempting to shift the debate. We are the civic participants formally known just as voters. All of this new activity is exhilarating—and also frustrating.

As more voices clamor for our attention, the result isn't just more noise in the public arena and more emails flooding congressional inboxes. Mass participation by today's online activists through the dominant forms used to channel attention—email, blogs, and social media—is also contributing to governmental gridlock and more polarized politics. And it may be turning off a crucial portion of the electorate: people who don't have the time or inclination to join in daily political debate, as well as those who don't think the issues are all simply a matter of "us" versus "them."

This expansion of participation cuts across the political spectrum but is most visible at its edges. It started with Howard Dean in 2004 and flowered in 2008 with Barack Obama. More recently the "right roots" learned to master the new online platforms, especially after 2008, when the GOP lost its hold on Washington. On both sides, this new wave of digital politicking is driven by passionate ideologues. Over the last decade, the most popular political blogs in America have been the ones that serve partisan red meat to their readers. Likewise, the biggest email lists belong to groups with strong partisan agendas like MoveOn.org and FreedomWorks. And though many online activists use their platforms to unearth critical facts, user-generated media is also created and shared to dramatize and exaggerate the other side's faults—to paint all Tea Partiers as racist or Obama supporters as anti-American. Being hyper-connected, it seems, is contributing to hyper-polarization.

Another paradoxical result of today's mass-participation politics may be lower overall turnout in many elections, allowing well-organized outliers to pick up seats that otherwise might never tilt so hard to either side of the spectrum. As more such candidates eat up precious media attention, the result may be a self-reinforcing cycle of lower turnout and more victories by ideological candidates. After all, in a noisy political environment, the best way to stand out is to be outspoken. After Republican Congressman Joe Wilson shouted "You lie" at President Obama during his September 2009 address to a joint session of Congress on health care reform, he raised $1.8 million in campaign contributions in the following week (his Democratic opponent raised about $1.6 million).[42]

Why hasn't politics in America changed much for the better since the rise of the Internet? While it might be tempting to simply blame the Supreme Court's *Citizens United* decision of 2010, which loosened the floodgates of big money spending on so-called "independent expenditures" aimed at influencing the outcomes of elections, there really hasn't been a dramatic change in the importance of big money in American politics since then. It was dominant before *Citizens United*, and it remains dominant.

It's also worth noting that in the 2012 elections, hundreds of millions of dollars were spent by so-called SuperPacs to little avail. Some of those organizations devoted the bulk of their money on losers, as my colleagues at the Sunlight Foundation revealed.[43] Others, like the Credo Action SuperPac, used their much smaller war-chests to much greater effect. It isn't just having big money that gives you power in politics, it is how strategically you spend it.

There are three interrelated reasons, in my view, that the Internet hasn't changed politics as much as we imagined it would. First, at least in America, the successful and effective use of technology in politics no longer has a low barrier to entry. "Big data" may be cheaper to gather, but it is not cheaper to use effectively. Campaigns and activists have logically responded to the rise of online mass participation by developing and refining sophisticated and expensive techniques that enable them to manage inputs from larger numbers of people. But these responses tend to reinforce the power of insiders and elites, both old and new, as we shall see in the next two chapters on Big Data and Big Email, which will examine how digital technologies are changing electoral campaigns and political advocacy.

At the same time, the economics of staying independent aren't nearly as favorable as once imagined; most serious independent political bloggers have either been absorbed into mainstream media; joined together in group blogs that allow each individual to make a living elsewhere; or shut down. So while we continue to see new voices and initiatives appearing all the time—because the barrier to *entry* is lower—the challenge of keeping such independent efforts going often leads to more conventional outcomes. Centrality in the networked public sphere is going to those actors who have the resources to make themselves into attention-concentrating hubs.

Less visibly, the "world wide web" is no longer as open as it was a decade ago. Of the top fifty most trafficked websites, only one—Wikipedia—is run by a nonprofit organization. And the most popular sites, platforms like Facebook and Google, have largely succeeded in getting their billions of users to trade convenience for autonomy, converting once-free netizens into eyeballs and data to be sold to advertisers. For example, Facebook, which is essentially just a publishing platform like any other blogging service—albeit one that is incredibly well-designed and easy to use—no longer automatically shares what a user posts with all of their friends. If you want one of your Facebook posts to be read by all of your followers, you have to pay Facebook a premium for that privilege.[44]

In this, and many other subtle ways, the great democratizing potential of the networked public sphere is being throttled and walled off. Simultaneously, because they have become like utilities that everyone uses, companies like Facebook and Google have gained tremendous new capabilities to shape public awareness and behavior, with little transparency into exactly how they may be using those powers, as will be discussed in the Big Data chapter of the book.

Second, as indicated above, in an environment of increasingly dispersed attention, the Internet is much better at gathering "stop" energy than it is at building "go" energy. New voices are definitely entering the public conversation, but protests and campaigns led by free agents generally do not get converted into ongoing movements for change. For example, the ten to twenty million people who called and emailed Congress to stop the SOPA and PIPA bills have not been organized on the ground in any substantial way, beyond loci of support in New York and San Francisco. This power is mostly latent: without another external stimulus as provocative as the SOPA and PIPA legislation, it may never coalesce again. And while big online organizations like MoveOn.org and its many cousins have shown that atomized individuals can be brought together to nimbly respond to breaking news, this strength is also still mostly reactive, as we shall see in the chapter on Big Email.

The architecture of participation that Big Email and common-interest blogs create is also contributing to the hollowing out of local, cross-ideological community interaction. While it is wonderful that it has become easier to "find the others" online—which can be a life-saving fact if you are an isolated gay teenager growing up in a conservative rural town, for example—the amount of time people now spend in online communities of similar interest may well be reducing the time they spend interacting with peers and neighbors. The trend is toward more "vertical" forms of political association than "horizontal" ones.

This produces a different kind of political organization, nimble and opportunistic, capable of responding quickly to breaking news when an issue is likely to generate a strong response from members, but less likely to have strong local chapters capable of pressuring political representatives in the same way as the National Rifle Association or local labor unions.

Finally, the "stop/go" gap points to the heart of our current problem: the tools we have for actually getting things done *together*, as opposed to protesting and attacking others, are woefully thin. Email lists, list-servs, wikis, blogs, and social media are used by billions of people and are great at enabling *self*-expression, but they're terrible at helping us collaborate in making decisions and reaching consensus. The primary strategies used by American advocacy groups and campaigns to attract and focus attention on their causes—optimizing the power of big email lists and fine-tuning social media tactics to make their content "go viral"—have the perverse effect of adding more noise to the entire media system. The digital arms race to build a bigger list or get more likes and shares is unwinnable.

The result is a body politic that has grown more and more distorted. It has a gigantic mouth and two huge fists, left and right, that spend most of their time swinging at each other. Its heart still beats strong, and often it races in response to emotional events. But its ears and eyes are deafened and blinded by all the noise and flash; its stomach only rarely gets to digest anything; and its leg muscles are atrophying from lack of use.

We can save the body politic, but to do so we must remember that the purpose of democracy isn't only for each of us to have our say, but to blend individual opinions into common agreements. Instead of letting our digital tools drive us in ways that exacerbate our differences, we must insist on tools that bring us together as equals to solve problems.

Interestingly enough, the Internet's own early engineers understood this challenge very well. "We reject: kings, presidents and voting," said David Clark at the 1992 meeting of the Internet Engineering Task Force. "We believe in: rough consensus and running code."[45] His words are as relevant today as they were then.

We must also take active steps to restore a real balance of power between citizens and the state, and citizens and the private enterprises that host and profit from our digital lives. The pendulum between privacy and convenience has swung too far to one side, as we Americans have allowed our government to make drastic, unconstitutional, and secret incursions into our private lives through digital monitoring.

The gigantic economy that has been built by online platforms collecting, merging, and selling our data needs to be curbed by a mix of governmental restrictions and individual changes in how we conduct our own communications. We need a real digital public square, not one hosted by Facebook, shaped by Google, and monitored by the National Security Agency. If we don't build one, then any notion of democracy as "rule by the people" will no longer be meaningful. We will be a nation of Big Data, by Big Email, for the powers that be.

2

Big Data: The Politics of Computational Management

"The bottom up stuff needs to be enforced from the top down."
—Joe Rospars, digital director for the 2008 Obama
presidential campaign

As of Election Day 2012, Barack Obama's re-election campaign said its staff and volunteers called or knocked on the doors of 150 million voters—five times as many as it did in 2008.[1] Twenty-five million of those contacts were made in the last four days of the race, compared to just three million in the same time period four years earlier. The campaign said it counted 2.2 million volunteers who had worked a shift at some point during the long process. More than 358,000 offline campaign events were organized through the campaign's "Dashboard" tool, nearly double the number organized four years earlier using My.BarackObama. com. A whopping 4.4 million individuals made a donation to his war-chest, almost half a million more than the heady days of his first run. He accumulated more than thirty-two million "likes" on Facebook, thirteen times the number he had on Election Day 2008.[2] And most amazing: the campaign collected the email addresses of thirty million people, almost half his actual vote total of 65 million.[3] By comparison, the Obama campaign email list from 2008 totaled "just" thirteen million.

Both the 2008 and 2012 Obama presidential campaigns were digital juggernauts, and professionals inside and outside of politics continue to study them for lessons in how to do everything from email fundraising and website optimization to personalized advertising and micro-targeted social media sharing. The question that should concern anyone wondering about the health of our democracy, as opposed to the method-ology of modern marketing, is how is it that all this Internet-enabled participation has produced so little in terms of actual civic capacity?

There is nothing bigger than an American presidential cam-paign, in terms of how many ordinary people get swept into vol-unteering, organizing, and mobilizing to win a political contest. And yet it is painfully clear that for all its technological savvy and data-driven organizing, the Obama campaigns have not produced any change in the structure of the American people whatsoever. Voter turnout, the one bellwether that everyone likes to cite, dropped from 62.3 percent of the eligible electorate in 2008 to 57.5 percent in 2012.[4] And despite all the donations, volunteering, "likes," and "follows," we are just as disconnected from each other, in terms of civic capital, as we were before Obama swept onto the American stage.

There may have been a sea change in the number of Americans going online and joining social networks between

2004 and today, but the single biggest political organizer of our time, Barack Obama, the president of the United States, built very little local capacity. If he had, congressional battles related to his political priorities might have turned out quite differently.

Why did Obama's use of the Internet turn out to mainly empower him and his lieutenants, instead of also empowering his base? And where are these digital innovations taking American electoral politics? To answer these questions, we need to look back at how online political strategists have adapted to the rise of the web, starting with the first major presidential campaign of the Networked Age, that of Howard Dean.

Figure 2, located on page 235, is a screenshot of the Dean for America blog on October 9, 2003. This was close to the height of the Vermont governor's campaign for the presidency, as his poll numbers were approaching front-runner status. He had just wrapped up another record-breaking quarter of fundraising. The blog was the campaign's online heart, with a prominent link to it from the campaign's home page:

[See page 235.]

The actual blog content runs down the middle of the page. The top post, written at 1:09 AM by the campaign's chief blogger Mathew Gross, is an invitation for supporters to talk about whatever they want. "This is your space," he writes, echoing the Dean campaign's "You have the power" slogan. The previous post, from Wednesday night, is also an "open thread." Below that, there's an update on Iowa. Each of these posts has more than one hundred comments appended to them. Even in the middle of the night, thousands of people were coming to the Dean blog (a general rule of thumb for participation online: 90 percent of a site's visitors will just read; another 8 to 9 percent will occasionally post a comment or interact in some other way; and the bulk of activity comes from just one to 2 percent of a site's visitors).

On the right-hand column, or "rail," are a series of engagement tools: a link to a rally that day in Phoenix; a petition; an email signup box that advertises the current number of "Americans for Dean" (461,206); a link to the campaign's Meetup page (again, advertising the number of participants, 120,000); a link asking people to invite their friend to "join the campaign;" another one asking for contributions; downloadable posters; a link to "get local" and find other Dean events nearby; and a feedback button.

On the left-hand rail, there's a long series of links. The first bunch are for official campaign sites or functions, including "contribute"; "get local"; "DeanLink" (which allowed supporters to create their own online profile and link up with others); "Generation Dean" (the campaign's youth wing); "Dean for New Hampshire"; and a few calendar and publicity links. Then another set of links go to "featured sites" of various other subgroups being organized on behalf of the governor. And below that is the beginning of a long list of blogs, some run by individual writers supportive of the candidate and others representing local groups.

The full web page for that day's "Blog for America" is actually six screenshots long. It has many more links to "unofficial" Dean sites and blogs, along with more news from the campaign's bloggers about everything from new Meetups to a guest column from "Latinos for Dean" which lists dozens of local contact emails. Three screens down, there's another "overnight open thread," this one written at 1:07 AM by Joe Rospars, one of the campaign's bloggers. "What's on your mind?" he asks. "We're listening." A link takes you to the 407 comments this provoked.

This snapshot of the Dean campaign's online hub shows three things: online community was itself a value; the campaign wanted to maximize self-organization; and its staff didn't really know what they were doing, and so they tried everything. The campaign website was the center of a massive community conversation that drew tens of thousands of visitors, day and night. It wasn't just the standard billboard for the candidate's itinerary and press releases, with fundraising and list-building features. Supporters were invited to use the blog as a kind of digital watering hole for sharing ideas, inspiration, and feedback. Reading it, and seeing how others were interacting with it, gave Dean's supporters a tantalizing glimpse of their own collective mind at work. The blog page pointed outward to many official and unofficial campaign sites, sharing attention with and helping nurture a much larger network of supporters.

As University of North Carolina professor Daniel Kreiss writes in his recent book, *Taking Our Country Back: The Crafting of Networked Politics from Howard Dean to Barack Obama*, "Blog for America enabled the campaign to convene a community around the candidate in which supporters motivated each other, formed social ties, and reaffirmed their commitment to the candidate in the face of press or other candidate attacks. Comments on the blog, in turn, enabled Internet staffers to take the measure of supporters."[5] Joe Rospars told Kreiss, "The blog was used as the lifeline to the supporters. [Campaign manager Joe] Trippi spent a lot of time reading blog comments. . . . the center of gravity was the campaign blog."

The Dean website also gave its supporters a lot of capabilities for self-organization and self-expression. If you wanted to find out who else in your ZIP code had signed up as a Dean supporter, you could get many of their names from "Deanlink" and even send them an email. If you wanted to post an announcement about an upcoming event, you could just add a comment to the main blog. No major campaign in U.S. history had ever shared these kinds of bottom-up powers with their grassroots supporters. Things like supporter lists and messaging were heretofore tightly controlled.

However, the Dean site was a visual mess. It broke the first rule of good web design, which is to give a visitor just a few choices. The campaign's main home page was no better. Instead of the blog posts down the middle, it had campaign press releases. But it was just as cluttered with buttons, links, calls to action, "hot" items to click, the Meetup, Contribute, and Email signup options and much, much more, all displayed in a crazy quilt of typefaces and colors.

In retrospect, it is now clear that the Dean campaign represented the first full flowering of Internet-enabled mass participation in an American presidential contest. It is true that as presidential candidates in 2000, Senators Bill Bradley and John McCain each had surprising success with web-based fundraising. But back then relatively few Americans went online, self-publishing was in its infancy, and people were just getting accustomed to giving their credit card information to make online purchases or donations. This all changed in just a few years. In July of 2003, Technorati estimated there were half a million blogs in existence. That number was two million by March of 2004. It doubled again to four million by September.[6]

In 1996, presidential candidates Bill Clinton and Bob Dole had 130,000 and 140,000 small donors (people giving under $200), respectively. In 2000, Al Gore and George W. Bush had 120,000 and 110,000. The Internet and Americans' increasing comfort with online shopping changed that game: by 2004, campaign finance expert Michael Malbin estimates that Bush amassed about 1.1 million small donors, while John Kerry accumulated about 750,000.[7] Between 2000 and 2004, the number of small donors giving to the two major-party presidential candidates increased by more than 700 percent. These numbers were the most visible sign of a much larger wave of grass-roots activity in the political arena.

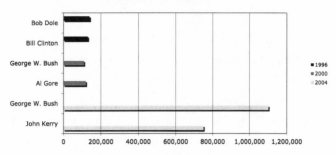

Number of small (under $200) donors to presidential candidates 1996-2004

Mass participation was something new. In early 2003, it meant that grassroots Democratic activists who were unhappy with their party's putative standard-bearers and angry at how many of its leaders in Congress were supporting President George W. Bush's push to war with Iraq could band together ("find the others") and search out their own alternative candidates to support. They met on blogs like MyDD.com and DailyKos.com, and started using Meetup.com—a free tool for coordinating local get-togethers—to start forming Howard Dean Meetups before the campaign even knew they existed. Thus it was possible for hundreds of Dean supporters to organize their own small-donor fundraising events in New York City in early 2003 and inveigle their way onto the candidate's schedule. When Dean, joined by Joe Trippi, walked up to the Essex bar on the Lower East Side and saw a line spilling out onto the street of people they had never seen before, the campaign's leadership realized that they had tapped into a new vein of political energy.

It looked as though the old-fashioned top-down campaign organizations of the TV-dominated era of American politics were on the verge of being replaced by something more bottom-up and open. Power seemed to be moving to the edges from the center, as activists popularized their own messages, created their own online organizing hubs, and pressed forward on issues that they thought were the most important.

And this phenomenon wasn't just emerging in American presidential politics. The rapid spread of anti-Iraq War protests around the U.S. and the rest of the world in early 2003, powered by online networks like MoveOn.org, led *The New York Times* to posit the emergence of a "second superpower"[8]—world public opinion—capable of challenging the Bush administration's push to war.

The Dean campaign did everything it could to fuel this sense of transformation, directing key staff to open up direct lines of communication with online communities like the website SmirkingChimp.com (a 20,000 member hotbed of anti-Bush sentiment); to interact extensively through the campaign blog; to channel activist suggestions for campaign tactics up the ladder to its Vermont campaign headquarters; and to give local Dean Meetups and independent pro-Dean groups and websites a great deal of freedom to do whatever they wanted on behalf of the candidate. At the center of this roiling stew was the blog, which, in the words of Mathew Gross, its primary author, became "a source of endless ideas and language." In *Mousepads, Shoe Leather and Hope*, a group memoir of the Dean campaign, he writes:

> *Some of the most memorable phrases ("The Tea Is in the Harbor!") and events (the July fund-raiser in which we raised $500,000 online by putting Howard Dean in front of a computer with a turkey sandwich, in contrast to the $2,000 a plate luncheon with Vice President Cheney that was taking place the same day) came from the community of supporters who interacted with the staff and each other in the burgeoning comment threads.[9]*

But the explosion of participation that the Internet made possible also created vast new challenges for Dean's political campaign. A lightning rod must be able to absorb and direct the energy that flows into it. All the veterans of the Dean campaign describe their experience trying to manage the volunteer offerings that cascaded their way as nearly impossible.

Nicco Mele, Dean's webmaster, told me that at one point during the campaign, more than 60,000 individual emails were sent to info@deanforamerica.com. And the campaign only had twelve volunteers tasked with responding. As a result, he deliberately made it harder for people to find that email address. "The real problem," he told me back then, "isn't all those people visiting the website; it's 600,000 people receiving an email from us and hitting reply, with the expectation of a response."[10] Presidential campaigns weren't designed to scale to that level of interactivity; nor was it even clear if it helped the campaign to be that responsive.

Now, fast-forward eight years to the home page of BarackObama.com on November 25, 2011:

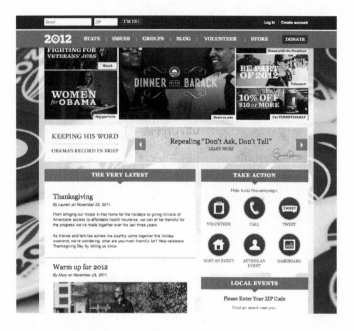

A lot has changed in campaign web design, signifying all kinds of hard-earned wisdom about how to use the Internet in presidential campaigns. The biggest change is how few words and links there are on this page compared to the Dean site from 2003. All of that clutter has been replaced by a unified visual palette that channels the visitor to four or five key options for his or her attention: a series of headlined opportunities to learn about the candidate or "be part" of the campaign by donating or volunteering; a plug for the candidate's record on an issue of current import; some bite-sized news from the campaign ("the very latest"); a mini-portal offering a few key ways to "take action"; and a button inviting people to find local events near them.

There are no links pointing outward to bloggers or other unofficial campaign sites. Nor is there any invitation to hang out and join in a conversation, though the Obama blog does allow for comments. Instead, the 2012 Obama website offers visitors a streamlined experience: you can use it to learn a little bit more about the candidate, or you can use it to do a few things the campaign wants you to do: sign up, volunteer, make calls, donate, host an event, attend an event, or tweet out the message of the moment. Unlike Dean, the 2012 Obama campaign website is not trying to foster any kind of national political community, either on its pages or by sharing attention with supporter sites elsewhere. It is a highly functional portal for gathering information, money, and time from campaign supporters. Self-organization and self-expression by Obama supporters are not its concern.

In short, between the 2004 and 2012 presidential campaigns in the United States, online campaign strategists made a series of critical decisions about how best to use the web to win political campaigns. Their goals didn't change: to raise money, to identify supporters and volunteers, to spread their candidate's message, and ultimately to get out their voters. But their methods adapted in critical ways.

In 2004, campaigners were open to everything. As the Dean campaign showed, they were willing to give their supporters a lot of attention and freedom, reasoning that if they built a vibrant sense of community online and offline, it would generate more money and volunteering. And it worked: Dean raised a record $51 million in 2003, and nearly 40 percent of that came from small donation amounts of less than $200.[11] Additionally, after his loss, he converted his 600,000-person email list and 1,000 local Dean Meetups into a political action committee called Democracy for America, which under his brother Jim's leadership has since grown to a million members with dozens of local chapters and has helped recruit, train, and elect more than 600 like-minded candidates to local office. That move by Dean shows that it was possible to convert the energies of campaign volunteers into long-term political organizing. But as we shall see, what Dean did was highly unusual.

The End of a Disruptive Era

Between 2004 and 2012, as massive new social networking and sharing platforms such as YouTube, Facebook, and Twitter became dominant, online political campaigners began to refine their practices. The content and services offered on campaign websites was steadily reduced, while digital campaign teams got better at using those sites and related tools to collect information on visitors. Instead of trying to empower voters and volunteers with a broad range of tools and capabilities, campaigns focused on better managing them.

Internet organizer Judith Freeman worked on John Kerry's general election online campaign in 2004 and then served as the new media field manager for Obama's 2008 campaign. In between, she co-founded the New Organizing Institute, a key training center for Democrats and progressives. She addressed the shift this way:

I think that is one of the biggest lessons that we learned in 2004—and they obviously did it way better in 2008 then they did it in 2004—if you don't create a structure and give people a way to get engaged people are going to figure it out on their own. They are going to create their own Google groups or their own neighborhood block party, or whatever. And so it is up to you as a campaign, especially a presidential campaign, where everyone wants to get involved, to create the structures and give people ways to get engaged and help the campaign with their strategy. Otherwise everyone is just going to be running around doing anything.[12]

Speaking at the Personal Democracy Forum Europe conference in 2009 in Barcelona, Joe Rospars—who had just finished running Obama's successful 2008 online campaign—put it much more bluntly. "The bottom up stuff needs to be enforced from the top down," he declared.[13]

In 2008, My.BarackObama.com (or MyBO for short), the Obama campaign's innovative social networking platform, not only gave supporters the ability to create local events and fundraise, it also enabled them to form groups, affiliate with friends, and even blog. Bits of "DeanLink," with its group-forming capability, and "DeanSpace," a knock-off of MySpace that allowed supporters to create their own profile pages, lived on in MyBO circa 2008. That was no accident—some of the code had been written by developers working for the Dean campaign who then formed the Blue State Digital technology consulting firm, a firm which won the Obama campaign account in 2007.

They had continued to tinker with their online organizing software even before Obama started running in 2007, building platforms for the Democratic National Committee (called "Partybuilder") and for a network of state-based progressives called Progress Now.

The DNA from the Dean campaign was also carried into the 2008 Obama web platform because the Obama campaign believed its supporters expected it to offer them a state-of-the-art toolset. The campaign also wanted to draw its supporters away from third-party services like MySpace or Facebook and onto its own platform, so it would have more access to their data and more control over their activities. That included literally demanding that a popular Obama MySpace page created and managed by a volunteer for several years before Obama started his campaign for president be handed over to the campaign's online organizing team. This infamous incident was seen by mainline "netroots" activists as indicative of a much more controlling approach.[14]

In 2008, the Obama campaign still treated its campaign blog as an important communications tool. But the open and freewheeling style of the Dean blog was replaced by something far more carefully calibrated to the campaign's needs.

As Kreiss describes, "Rospars wanted the blog to become the 'voice of the grassroots movement' by highlighting the work of supporters and articulating the reasons they backed Obama."[15] Campaign blogger Sam Graham-Felsen understood that his job was to tell two stories via the blog—how Obama was "this great man of hope and change" and how he was "a community organizer" devoted to building power "from the bottom up." But the blog wasn't the place for riling up supporters with jabs at the other candidates, or for connecting grass-roots volunteers to the campaign staff in any meaningful way. It was a performance space for projecting the image the Obama campaign wanted people to see.

To enable Graham-Felsen to sustain this image of community, Kreiss reports, Rospars isolated him and the other campaign bloggers from other aspects of the campaign operation. He writes:

> To protect a very fragile suspension of disbelief in the authenticity of the Obama campaign and its supporters, Rospars repeatedly told Graham-Felsen to 'stay in this bubble [with supporters] and not get too close to the sausage making and all this other stuff.' In other words, Rospars insulated Graham-Felsen from much of the day-to-day work of the campaign and the New Media Division. This was the work . . . that helped give rise to and coordinate supporter participation, from targeting persuasive communication to processing enormous amounts of data on the electorate. Indeed, Graham-Felsen attributes his belief in

the campaign as a supporter-driven movement, as well as the way that he wrote and acted as if everyone else shared this belief, to this sequestering. As such, the ability of Graham-Felsen to represent the campaign as a supporter-driven movement was contingent upon his removal from the complicated, day-to-day strategizing and data work that challenged overly romantic narratives of Obama's run.[16]

Even with those limitations, in 2008, Obama supporters used the tools the campaign gave them to do a lot of self-organizing, swept up in the massive cult of personality that the Obama campaign adroitly encouraged and benefited from. Two million people created profiles on MyBO; 200,000 local events were planned using the site's tools; more than 35,000 volunteer groups were created; and about 400,000 blog posts were written. Perhaps most valuable, about 70,000 people created their own fundraising pages on MyBO, raising $30 million from their own networks of family, friends, and acquaintances.[17]

However, by 2012, when the Obama campaign unveiled a completely retooled "Dashboard" for its volunteers, most of the self-organizing features prevalent in 2008 had been removed. Instead of giving supporters the ability to connect with friends, organize events, message each other, form groups, start fundraising mini-campaigns, and blog, the 2012 Dashboard sought mainly to funnel people into local neighborhood teams. Signing up meant entering your address, setting up a personal profile, and then being propelled into joining your local team, where you could report on how often you did things like canvassing or making phone calls on behalf of the campaign.

Dashboard still allowed people to form groups or launch their own fundraising pushes, and it also allowed people to post their own updates, Facebook-style, either to their individual group, or in response to messages on the campaign's national news feed. But those conversations were buried several layers deep on the Obama campaign website. They were not considered central to the campaign's message or organizing efforts. What was important was getting people sorted into the right local group where they could be engaged by a field organizer and where their activities could be tracked and fine-tuned according to the outputs most desired by the campaign's managers. As writer Nancy Scola put it, "For a campaign that eats metrics for breakfast and data for lunch," this was where the action was.[18]

Kreiss calls this set of practices "computational management" and locates its initial emergence in the new media division of the 2008 Obama campaign under Rospars. He writes, "Data lay behind decisions of where to allocate resources, how to staff and organize new media work, and grounded claims for resources from the larger campaign organization and the authority of the Division. The Division's leadership conducted rigorous analysis of the returns on investment that every new media expenditure produced, from dollars to voter registrations, to both be efficient in its own work and to garner organizational resources."

The Obama campaign moved in this direction because the very technology it was using—email solicitations, web forms, cookies—lent itself so seamlessly to data collection and analysis. Or as one unnamed new media staffer told Kreiss, "The Division could do this because, unlike other media, online media 'is a closed loop, you can measure from displays to clicked versions with no, basically zero externality, because it happens so accurately—the measurement is enough.'"[19]

The important thing to remember about computational management is that it reinforces, in multiple ways, the power of a political campaign's staff as opposed to its supporters. In 2004, grassroots Dean activists seized on available technologies like blogs and Meetup.com to organize beyond the campaign's formal structure. In 2008, some people did similar things using YouTube or Facebook to popularize their own independent messages about candidates, or to form their own groups, some of which were then drawn into official campaign structures. But by 2012, these citizen-led developments were outpaced by the complexity and sophistication of the Obama campaign's use of data and analytics to do everything from test email subject lines and website landing pages to scripting the conversations of field operatives knocking on doors, and targeting messages to individual voters in key states.

"What new media have not done is to necessarily make candidates more responsive to their mobilized supporters," writes Kreiss. "The use of new media in campaigning has seemingly not brought about fundamental changes in the levers of accountability, forms of political representation, quality of democratic conversation, or distribution of power in the American polity."[20]

The managers of Obama's massive campaign apparatus never intended to turn their operation into anything else; they merely saw it as a tool whose levers they controlled. If the McCain campaign of 2008 was the last 20th century top-down campaign, the Obama campaign was the first 21st century version. For David Plouffe, Obama 2008's campaign manager, the gigantic email list, its millions of donors, and its vibrant online social network were essentially a new kind of broadcast system, one even better than TV. Near the end of his election memoir, *The Audacity to Win*, he writes:

> *Our e-mail list had reached thirteen million people. We had essentially created our own television network, only better, because we communicated with no filter to what would amount to about 20 percent of the total number of votes we would need to win ... And those supporters would share our positive message or response to an attack, whether through orchestrated campaign activity like door-knocking or phone calling or just in conversations they had each day with friends, family, and colleagues.[21]*

This worked as long as the Obama campaign and its support base were united around the same goal of getting him elected. But that thirteen-million-member email list turned out to be a much weaker force once Obama was in the White House, and his political operatives tried to use it to support his agenda. In the new age of mass participation, action only flows out of genuine concern. You can't order volunteers to do anything they don't want to do. People have minds of their own.

To many people who supported Obama in 2008, or wished him well, this collapse in grass-roots organizing strength remains an unresolved mystery. After all, the need to keep the pressure on Congress from outside Washington was a constant refrain in Obama's speeches as he campaigned. "The more we can enlist the American people to pay attention and be involved, that's the only way we are going move an agenda forward," Obama declared at a spring 2008 campaign rally in Indianapolis. "That's how we are going to counteract the special interests." He added, "And one of the things that I'm most proud about in this campaign is that we've built a structure that can sustain itself after the campaign."[22]

The myth of the Obama campaign as a bottom-up enterprise powered by millions of small donors, grassroots volunteers, local field organizers, and the Internet was assiduously cultivated, both during and after his election. And the press never inquired very deeply into the truth of that myth. Instead, we got a stream of laudatory profiles.

Here are some quotes from *Rolling Stone*'s March 2008 story "The Machinery of Hope"[23]:

- "The Obama campaign has shattered the top-down, command-and-control, broadcast-TV model that has dominated American politics since the early 1960s. 'They have taken the bottom-up campaign and absolutely perfected it,' says

Joe Trippi, who masterminded Dean's Internet campaign in 2004."

- "'When we started this race, Barack told us that he wanted the campaign to be a vehicle for involving people and giving them a stake in the kind of organizing he believed in,' [chief campaign strategist David] Axelrod says. 'He is still the same guy who came to Chicago as a community organizer twenty-three years ago. The idea that we can organize together and improve our country—I mean, he really believes that.'"

- "'We put these tools online as a public utility,' says Joe Rospars . . .'We said to our supporters,' 'Have at it.'"

- "'Obama didn't just take their money,' says Donna Brazile, Al Gore's campaign manager in 2000. 'He gave them seats at the table and allowed them to become players.'"

From *Fast Company*'s March 2009 cover story on Chris Hughes, the Facebook cofounder who led the development of MyBO, headlined "The Kid Who Made Obama President"[24]:

- "'Technology has always been used as a net to capture people in a campaign or cause, but not to organize,' says Obama campaign manager David Plouffe. 'Chris saw what was possible before anyone else.'"

- "The theme of the campaign, direct from Obama, was that the people were the organization."

- ". . . the community-organizer candidate wanted a nation of organizers, and Hughes made that happen."

- "Trusting a community can produce dramatic and unexpected results."

From *National Journal*'s April 2009 profile[25] of Joe Rospars, the Obama campaign's new media director:

- ". . . after he met with Plouffe and Obama, Rospars saw an opportunity to run a campaign in a unique way. 'It was going to be something organic. It was going to be bottom-up,' Joe Rospars said."
- "'At the core of our campaign were the grassroots supporters, and they would be the main reason we won,' Plouffe recalls. 'They came through the Internet and organized online. They were the heartbeat of our campaign, and Joe and his team realized that.'"

And from *Esquire*'s March 2009 capstone story on Obama campaign manager David Plouffe, "The Man Who Made Obama"[26]:

- Obama owned the web because Plouffe believed in a few smart kids and let them go a little nuts.
- It was Plouffe who gathered the president's unprecedented thirteen-million-name contact list, which has grown into a fulsome pulsing beast, and it is Plouffe who now owns it and keeps it under lock and key. Plouffe sent those thirteen million people an e-mail in mid-November and they replied, Yes, I still want to be involved, and yes, David Plouffe, I'll

have house parties when you tell me to. Here is who I am socioeconomically and socially. I am boxers; my next-door neighbor is briefs. Now the president has instructed him to make that list a new lever of government. . . . The idea is a national operation, likely named Organizing for America, that will resemble Obama's grassroots operation in reach and love. It will be as finely tuned as the campaign behemoth and funded the same way—no money from third parties. If Obama has a policy initiative he wants to push, or a message he needs to disseminate, or a gaffe he wants to bat down, he will call David Plouffe and Plouffe will unleash the many-million-mouthed dog, just as he did all across America for these past two years.

Indeed, after the 2008 victory, the Obama campaign surveyed its massive email list, and more than a half million people reportedly responded. Two-thirds said that not only were they interested in helping the president pass his legislative agenda, they believed it was important to elect state and local candidates to advance the goals of the campaign. And more than 50,000 said they personally were interested in running for local office. A follow-on organization, Organizing for America, was created to support the president's agenda. But no significant resources flowed into local organizing. In contrast to Dean's Democracy for America group, which has nurtured a few hundred candidacies, those 50,000 candidates inspired by Obama's first election victory never materialized.

Why not? The tools and information the Obama campaign gave its volunteers were designed to help him get elected, *not to help them stay self-directed.* Unlike the meticulous planning done for the transition into power in Washington, there was no plan for how to transition the grass-roots energy of the campaign until months after it was over. In the fall of 2008, a side effort by some Obama tech volunteers to start work on a website to capture and channel grassroots passion in the event he won was kyboshed by campaign insiders. And the process for managing that organizational transition was as closed and controlled as the campaign itself.

"Is this really what 'building on the movement to elect Barack Obama' is going to look like?" Marshall Ganz, the brilliant long-time community organizer who trained many of Obama's field organizers, asked at the time. Ganz commented, "I can't believe this was put out by the same people who trained organizers in how to do house meetings in the campaign over the past two years."[27]

Worse yet, what came out of that process was not a grassroots army geared up to march on Washington for change, but a hobbled and tamed tiger. Jessica Shearer, a veteran of labor organizing who ultimately managed the field operations in nine key states for Obama in 2008, said later that the Obama team had basically "kneecapped" their grassroots after the 2008 victory. "The list that the Obama campaign put together is the best list in history," she said, referring to the Obama for America email list. "That is a list that is truly representative, that is deep in all kinds of communities across this country. If [Howard] Dean had been put in charge of the Democratic Party after that election, that list might have really built the democracy. It might have built a party. It might have allowed people a place to engage. Instead, it was this weak echo chamber, where they couldn't be one step to the left or one step to the right of anything the president said."[28]

But while the most active volunteers on the Obama campaign were indeed given a fair amount of autonomy to make decisions about how to organize in their precincts during the election fight, afterwards they had no agency. Writing in 2010, Sam Graham-Felsen, the chief blogger on the Obama campaign who did such a good job conveying the image of Obama as community organizer and his movement as grassroots, pointed out how badly the White House had botched the opportunity:

> . . . one reason the White House has struggled is because this kind of approach towards the grassroots hasn't carried over to the administration. The people on Obama's thirteen-million-person email list have been asked to sign e-cards for Obama's birthday and buy souvenir mugs . . . They could have been asked to take action that requires sacrifice and struggle—like pressuring the Democratic Senators who stood, for so long, in the way of passing health care reform. Instead, they've been told to voice soft, inoffensive support for Obama's initiatives, to essentially keep quiet while the President's inner circle negotiates with Congress behind closed doors.[29]

The person Obama, Axelrod, and Plouffe chose to take the central role of White House Chief of Staff, Rahm Emanuel, was known to be a consummate inside player with a strong disdain for the Democratic party's grassroots and netroots activists. Big liberal interest groups were kept in check by promises of access and requests for patience until it was time for their issue to be addressed. And when people broke that discipline, the White House punished them. After Steve Hildebrand, the deputy campaign manager in 2008, spoke out the next summer about "losing patience"[30] with the White House's cautious approach toward everything from health care reform to gay marriage, word spread to the press of his battles with depression.[31]

Marshall Ganz summarized what went wrong in November 2010, the day after Obama suffered a catastrophic rebuke in the Congressional elections and lost control of the House of Representatives:

"Transformational" leadership engages followers in the risky and often exhilarating work of changing the world, work that often changes the activists themselves. Its sources are shared values that become wellsprings of the courage, creativity and hope needed to open new pathways to success. "Transactional" leadership, on the other hand, is about horse-trading, operating within the routine, and it is practiced to maintain, rather than change, the status quo.

The nation was ready for transformation, but the president gave us transaction. And, as is the case with leadership failures, much of the public's anger, disappointment and frustration has been turned on a leader who failed to lead.

Obama and his team made three crucial choices that undermined the president's transformational mission. First, he abandoned the bully pulpit of moral argument and public education. Next, he chose to lead with a politics of compromise rather than advocacy. And finally, he chose to demobilize the movement that elected him president. By shifting focus from a public ready to drive change—as in "yes we can"—he shifted the focus to himself and attempted to negotiate change from the inside, as in "yes I can."

. . . Finally, the president demobilized the widest, deepest and most effective grass-roots organization ever built to support a Democratic president. With the help of new media and a core of some 3,000 well-trained and highly motivated organizers, 13.5 million volunteers set the Obama campaign apart. They were not the "usual suspects"—party loyalists, union staff, and paid canvassers—but a broad array of first-time citizen activists. Nor were they merely an e-mail list. At least 1.5 million people, according to the campaign's calculations, played active roles in local leadership teams across the nation.

But the Obama team put the whole thing to sleep, except for a late-breaking attempt to rally support for healthcare reform. Volunteers were exiled to the confines of the Democratic National Committee. "Fighting for the president's agenda" meant doing as you were told, sending redundant e-mails to legislators and responding to ubiquitous pleas for money. Even the touted call for citizen "input" into governance consisted mainly of e-mails, mass conference calls and the occasional summoning of "real people" to legitimize White House events.[32]

This is not to say that voters lost all agency between 2004 and 2012 as the Internet became a central playing field for American politics and campaigns learned to adapt. In 2008, voter-generated content on social media altered the trajectory of the campaign several times, and it made sense to pay attention to how activist voters were using the web and social media to try to influence the campaign.

There were several breakout moments that came from independent Internet-powered organizing: on Facebook, the "Million Strong for Barack"[33] and "Million Strong Against Hillary Clinton"[34] groups really did gather a million supporters while operating outside the control of the campaigns. Phil de Vellis's "Vote Different"[35] YouTube video disrupted Hillary Clinton's early push in 2007, and the "Dear Mr. Obama"[36] video from a wounded Iraq veteran spread a pro-McCain message and garnered more than ten million views late in 2008. One-day fundraising drives called "money-bombs" that were organized by Ron Paul's grassroots supporters really did break records. At one point, 20,000 people came together on MyBO itself to demand that their candidates "Get FISA Right,"[37] which actually forced the Obama to respond to direct criticism of his flip-flop on the warrantless wiretapping issue, putting this topic higher on the national agenda, albeit briefly.

In 2008 social media was still relatively new: people who were active in online networks tended to also be the most politically influential offline. If these hyper-active people were aligning with particular candidates or talking about them online, those choices and conversations seemed to have the potential to alter the dynamics of the race. At techPresident.com, the site I edit, we tracked those metrics carefully, and by the end of the campaign, we thought they were astounding: Barack Obama had 2,397,253 friends on Facebook to John McCain's 622,860. He had 125,639 Twitter followers to McCain's 5,319. There were 79,613 blog posts using the phrase "voting for Obama" compared to 42,093 saying "voting for McCain."[38] And these benchmarks were signifiers of a mass movement that involved millions of people participating in the election in a whole new way—not just on behalf of Obama, but on behalf of their own interests and causes.

But by 2012, it made less sense to pay close attention to social media metrics. The number of "likes" that Obama or Romney had on Election Day was of little more than academic interest. And the reason we stopped tracking these numbers is also why we were not interested by the campaigns' pages on new platforms like Tumblr, Pinterest, Instagram, or Spotify, and why we took a critical view of the Facebook "townhalls," Google "hangouts," Twitter "chats," and YouTube "ask the candidate" pages that popped up in 2012. Not one of these things had any real effect on the course of the election or caused the campaigns to engage the voters in any but the most superficial ways—though sadly that didn't stop the mainstream political media from wasting thousands of column inches covering their existence.

Social media didn't matter in 2012, except as a new form of passing entertainment, a temporary cure for boredom. The fact that the phrase "horses and bayonets" got the most mentions on Twitter during the third presidential debate won't even merit being a trivia question, but during 2012 that was the kind of story that social media tended to produce.[39] Momentary fame for the creator of the "binders full of women" Tumblr meant nothing in terms of generating any real political power for its creator, once the buzz faded a few days later.[40] It's true that the media operations of both campaigns worked hard to "win" every news cycle, and they worried about how social media could sometimes amplify small gaffes into larger stories.[41] But as political scientists[42] and data crunchers from Nate Silver[43] on down showed, these episodes had little lasting impact on voter opinions.

It's not that outside groups and freelance activists stopped trying to put new issues on the agenda using the networked public sphere. They were operating in a seemingly far more fertile environment, given the rapid adoption of social media by Americans. As the Pew Internet & American Life Project reported in October 2012, nearly 40 percent of all American adults said they had used sites like Facebook and Twitter to post about issues, link to political content, attempt to influence others, join political groups, or follow politicians. Two-thirds of people under the age of 29 said they did at least one of these things in 2012, roughly double what they were four years earlier.

So why were there so few breakout moments for voter-generated content in 2012? In 2008, both the Democratic and Republican fields were wide open, giving voters somewhat more leverage especially during the early part of the primary process. In 2012, Obama was running unopposed on the Democratic side of the aisle, which meant that there was little reason for anyone to pay attention to independent efforts to challenge him via social media. The electorate was also quite polarized in 2012, with most voters making up their minds fairly early with respect to who they were voting for. 2012 was also a less friendly environment for disruptive messages, with less of a public appetite for alternative views.

But voter-generated content also mattered less in 2012 because with mass participation comes greater cacophony, and in a bigger ocean it's harder to make a ripple. By August of 2012, there were more than two billion views of videos mentioning Obama or any of the Republican presidential candidates[44], a half-billion more than the entire 2008 cycle.[45] Surveys also showed that voter enthusiasm was down compared to 2008, especially among younger people who are often the seedbed for so many political movements. Political movements need a sense of urgency and romance; in 2012 support for Obama or Romney looked like a job, not an adventure.

There is one more complicated reason why voters using social media had comparatively less impact on the 2012 cycle: the campaigns and the tech platforms like Facebook, Twitter, and Google had learned something, which is how to monitor and channel online social media usage to their own advantage. The campaigns had discovered that if they "flooded the zone" with official content, they made it harder for voter-generated content to gain attention. They realized that there were potential benefits to be tapped from all the data they could collect from social media usage, such as the ability to better target their efforts to mobilize and persuade voters. But they shied away from using the full interactive potential of the web.

The Project on Excellence in Journalism (PEJ) took a close look at the Obama and Romney campaigns' use of their blogs, Facebook, Twitter, and YouTube channels and the level of social media response this usage generated over a two week period in early June 2012. What they found is that their use of these tools was highly controlled and generated a relatively weak response:

> *In theory, digital technology allows leaders to engage in a new level of "conversation" with voters, transforming campaigning into something more dynamic, more of a dialogue, than it was in the 20th century. For the most part, however, the presidential candidates are using their direct messaging mainly as a way*

to push their messages out. Citizen content was only minimally present on Romney's digital channels. The Obama campaign made more substantial use of citizen voices—but only in one area: the "news blog" on its website where that content could be completely controlled.

Of course, companies like Facebook, Google, and Twitter could have used their power as new media platforms to press the campaigns to behave differently. But they went along with the demands of these campaigns, choosing to create highly controlled online events that politicians felt comfortable embracing rather than making fuller use of all the possible interactive capabilities of the web. Both sides benefited: the politicians got a little "Internet buzz" for their appearances, and the tech companies got some cheap marketing. With a few exceptions, the political reporters who covered the election went merrily along for the ride.

It's the Data, Stupid

So much for the hope, expressed by many over the last ten years, that the era of top-down, highly managed, money-intensive presidential campaigns was ending. In 2012, the voters, once again, were channeled and controlled. The Internet's disruptive moment in presidential campaigns was effectively over. Instead, we have entered the age of data-driven campaigns and micro-targeted messaging and mobilization. He or she who masters data and analytics will rule.

In 2012, that was the billion-dollar Obama re-election campaign, which spent more than $100 million directly on technology to reach five million hard-to-contact young voters through their friends on Facebook (a program called "Targeted Sharing"), to run tens of thousands of simulations to gauge the effectiveness of their digital outreach programs, to model the likely behavior of tens of millions of voters in all the swing states, and to poll tens of thousands of voters a night. While the precision of all this work has been exaggerated, it undoubtedly helped the Obama campaign at the margins, allowing it to deploy volunteer canvassers more effectively and to spend TV advertising dollars more efficiently.

The campaign knew that emails signed by the First Lady were more likely to be opened than ones from the President; it knew that actor George Clooney's name in an email subject line was especially effective at unlocking the purse strings of West Coast women in their forties;[46] it knew which of the four campaign principals (the President, the First Lady, the Vice President, and his spouse) did best with what local audiences and planned their travel schedules around that data;[47] it knew that "ugly" formatting in fundraising emails outperformed more conventional formatting and it knew when that gimmick stopped working; and it had a score for every voter it targeted, estimating their likelihood to vote and their persuadability.[48]

If you were on Facebook and signed up to use the Obama campaign's "I'm In" app, you gave the campaign access to your basic info, including your name, picture, gender, birthday, religious affiliation, and political views. It also got permission to post status messages, notes, photos, and videos on your behalf and, most importantly, the ability to access your data even when you were not using the app (Facebook once prevented third-party apps from keeping any of that data, but that rule was dropped by the time of the 2012 cycle).[49] About a million people signed up. Through its "Targeted Sharing" program, the campaign figured out which of your Facebook friends were voters it needed to persuade, and then asked those supporters to push content through their posts and therefore onto their friends' Facebook newsfeeds. Because this content came from trusted sources—people's friends—the campaign found that people were more than twice as likely to click on it than on regular online banner ads.[50]

"We could [predict] people who were going to give online," a top campaign official told *Time* magazine. "We could model people who were going to give through mail. We could model volunteers."[51] The political campaign professionals and consultants who are establishing their own sophisticated approaches to data-intensive campaigning think this is great news. "This shit actually works" was the title of a packed panel on data-driven campaigns at RootsCamp 2012, an annual post-election gathering of progressive digital organizers that is hosted by the New Organizing Institute.[52] Academics and advocates who focus on the impact of political campaigns on our democratic fabric are less sanguine, fearing that we are entering a new age of data-intensive marketing and manipulation that will make the old days of direct mail and 30-second TV attack ads look like an New England town meeting.

This split view of the future impact of technology on American electoral politics kept people talking all year after the 2012 election cycle ended. Zeynep Tufekci, a professor of sociology at the University of North Carolina and former computer programmer, exemplified one pole of the debate. Noting the Obama campaign's expensive investment in technology and the tens of thousands of computer simulations the campaign ran daily, she wrote a widely read op-ed piece in *The New York Times* a few weeks after the election that asked, "What data, exactly, do campaigns have on voters? How exactly do they use it? What rights, if any, do voters have over this data, which may detail their online browsing habits, consumer purchases, and social media footprints?"

On top of that, she worried that campaigns would use their increasing powers of micro-targeting to "take persuasion into a private, invisible realm" where voters might be more easily manipulated by messages tailored to their personal interests and emotional weaknesses, and where the press, which is normally a partial check on sneaky campaign practices, would have few ways of fighting back. She warned that "these methods will also end up empowering better-financed campaigns," because "the databases are expensive, the algorithms are proprietary, the result of experiments by campaigns are secret, and the analytics require special expertise."[53]

Ethan Roeder, the data director for the Obama campaign, responded with his own op-ed in *The Times* a few weeks later. "Campaigns don't know anything more about your online behavior than any retailer, news outlet, or savvy blogger," he started. Of course, given how much retailers like Amazon, publishers, and the ad agencies who act as information brokers to the whole online commerce world actually collect and know about us, this is not entirely a reassuring statement. He went on to point out that, indeed, much of the data sifted by the Obama campaign was either provided voluntarily and directly by voters, or came from watching their clicks, which are generally trackable unless a user takes steps to anonymize their online behavior. Likewise, state voter files, which are the core building block of all campaign targeting, and which list basic information like a person's name, address, year of birth, party registration, and voting history, are public records. A great deal of the individual data that campaigns add to these databases and which allow them to micro-target individual voters comes from volunteers openly knocking on doors, making phone calls, and having one-on-one conversations with them. In other words, nothing the campaigns do with data is all that sneaky.

"The science of modeling is a modern-day application of a practice that has been around for nearly 200 years: polling," argued Roeder, explaining that:

> *Pollsters ask voters whom they support for president and how strongly. Campaigns then take demographic information about*

these voters into account in order to make assumptions about the entire population of a given state. The mechanics are exactly the same for public polls and internal campaign analyses. The difference is that the campaigns use statistical techniques to apply these assumptions to individual records in the voter file rather than stopping short and simply assuming that entire sections of the electorate will behave identically.

To him, the newly enlarged power of data-driven campaigns means that in the future, campaigns don't have to treat people as stereotypical groups like "Nascar dads" or "waitress moms" and can instead understand them as individuals.[54]

The debate between Tufekci and Roeder played out head-to-head when the two of them were on a panel together in May 2013 at a conference on "Data-Crunched Democracy" hosted by the Annenberg School at the University of Pennsylvania. Dressed in jeans and a T-shirt, Roeder was a scruffy, down-to-earth presence among the otherwise buttoned-up campaign consultants and academics who made up most of the audience. He began by agreeing that it was valid to worry about the Internet's impact on privacy in an age of Big Data. But he downplayed concerns about how it would be used by politicians. "Politicians exist to manipulate you," he said, with some vehemence, "and that is not going to change, regardless of how information is used." He continued:

OK, maybe we have a new form of manipulation, we have micro-manipulation, but what are the real concerns? What is the real problem that we see with the way information is being used? Because if it's manipulation, that ship has long since sailed. We are long past of the point of being able to design a political process that doesn't involve saying one thing to one group and another thing to another and attempting to leverage that difference to get as many votes as you possibly can.

He concluded: "Campaigns do not care about privacy. All campaigns care about is winning."[55]

When it was Tufekci's turn to speak, she didn't hold back either. The Turkish-born academic titled her talk "Engineering the Public," but she starting by joking that she had almost changed it to "I don't care where the rockets come down." That was a reference to an old satirical song by Tom Lehrer making fun of a former Nazi rocket scientist: "Once the rockets are up, who cares where they come down? That's not my department, says Wernher Von Braun." She was saying, with a touch of wry spunk, that today's campaign data scientists are building powerful new tools, but they don't seem to care about their larger impact on democracy.

"Political campaigns used to have this baseball bat called mass media," she pointed out. "Now they have a scalpel."[56] Not only that, it's one that can be wielded far less visibly, even tapping into the social networks of voters without their awareness. The Panopticon was the name that the philosopher Jeremy Bentham gave to a prison he designed where the inmates knew they were being watched, but not when, causing them to act as if they were being monitored constantly. "This is not the Panopticon," she noted, "because we don't know we're being watched." Tufekci repeated her fear that campaigns' new powers of computational modeling, when combined with new insights from behavioral science about how to manipulate voters' emotions, would further tilt the electoral playing field. Incumbents who can afford to collect this kind of data and deploy it effectively will have an advantage over poorly-resourced insurgents. And the growing ability to target people individually may allow powerful actors to hide their efforts from public scrutiny, further weakening the public sphere.

Finally, she warned that vast new powers were accruing to companies like Google, Twitter, and Facebook, the platforms on which so much of contemporary political discourse now takes place and the source of so much of the social and behavioral data that campaigns are starting to exploit. She ended her remarks by asking, "Could Facebook or Google swing an election?" The question hung over the room, unanswered.

Meet the New Bosses

In the old days of the 1960s, 70s and 80s, when politics was something the public learned about from one of the three main network television news programs, political reporters and pundits effectively decided what would lead the country's news agenda and which politicians should be taken seriously. Back then, we legitimately worried that some issues might be ignored or some candidates unfairly discouraged. But in the new media environment, might new platforms come to play a different but equally powerful role? Could a tech giant indeed swing an election?

We already know that these big platforms indeed have the power to influence people's voting behavior. A 2012 academic study published in *Nature* found that a non-partisan get-out-the-vote reminder on Facebook could increase voter turn-out—especially if it came with evidence that a user's real friends were also voting. Indeed, the report's authors estimated that about 340,000 additional people voted in America's 2010 congressional election because of the "I Voted" button that Facebook inserted on the pages of its American users on Election Day. Working with Facebook's cooperation, the researchers had access to 61 million Facebook users who were at least eighteen years old by Election Day 2010, hence the study's startling title: "A 61-million-person experiment in social influence and political mobilization."[57]

The experiment randomly divided people into three groups. The first group was about 60 million people (the "social message" group) who were shown a "get out the vote" message at the top of their News Feed, which included a link to local polling places, an "I Voted" button, a counter tallying how many other users had reported voting, and up to six profile pictures of their own Facebook friends who had reported voting. The second group of about 600,000 (the "informational message" group) were shown all of those things except the faces of their friends. The third group, also comprised of about 600,000 people, were a control group who were not shown any get-out-the-vote message at all. For about 10 percent of the overall group, the researchers were also able to validate their voting behavior from publicly available voter records after the election was over.

Users who received the social message were 2.08 percent more likely to say they voted than those who received the informational message without the pictures of their friends (that is, 20.04 percent vs 17.96 percent). They were about .4 percent more likely to have actually voted, based on the researchers' checking of voting records. More than twelve million people overall clicked on the "I Voted" button in 2010, compared to about 5.4 million in 2008.

The study's authors noted that, "seeing faces of friends significantly contributed to the overall effect of the message on real-world voting. In fact, turnout among those who received the informational message was identical to turnout among those in the control group . . . which raises doubts about the effectiveness of information-only appeals to vote in this context." People who saw pictures of close friends (determined by the amount they interacted with each other on Facebook) were more likely to be influenced positively. Party identification had no effect either way.

The study determined that "friends generated an additional 886,000 expressed votes" and "close friends generated a further 559,000 votes," but based on actual validation of people's voting, the verified impact of the Facebook message—the 340,000 additional votes noted above—was entirely due to the influence of close friends. "There is no evidence that ordinary friends had any effect on either [validated voting or polling place searches]. In other words, close friendships accounted for all of the significant contagion of these behaviors, in spite of the fact that they make up only 7 percent of all friendships on Facebook."

The authors noted that while these "contagion effects" are small, they only sent one message on Election Day, and the pool of people receiving it might have already voted by absentee ballot, or not logged into Facebook that day, or logged in too late to influence others. They also noted that they probably undercounted the number of actual votes influenced by the message because they couldn't match people's Facebook names to voter records due to typos, nicknames, and the like.[58]

This news turned heads in the political technology world, but it should have also been front-page news in mainstream media. But how would a reporter even verify these claims? How could *The New York Times* check that Facebook indeed did what it said it did on 61 million of its users' pages?

One of the least-noticed implications of our new age of data-intensive politics is that one side has nearly all the marbles. Until reporters and other observers develop the tools to independently monitor the uses of Big Data by third-party platforms (as well as by campaigns), the integrity of the process will rest entirely on the honesty of the data scientists and engineers inside these organizations. We already know that campaigns will do whatever they think they can get away with to win. Will massive publicly-traded corporations behave more ethically?

Let's assume that a well-designed nudge from Facebook can increase voter turnout by a modest, but measurable, degree, somewhere between .4 percent and 2 percent as reported in *Nature*. Now what if Facebook were to place that nudge only on pages of users who said they were Democrats?

Presumably someone would notice and sound the alarm. But what if the nudge was only on pages of Democrats in one key swing state? Or, what if the button was on everyone's page, but Facebook changed its News Feed feature to limit the sharing of that news to a targeted group? Would that kind of manipulation be as easy to uncover? The company already limits the number of users who will see something that someone posts randomly to their feed; you have to pay extra to "promote" it to everyone else. Might Facebook play favorites?

Now imagine this scenario: one day, a giant retailer, say, Wal-Mart, decides that it's going to let outside suppliers have special displays in a portion of their stores. They call this new service, "Wal-Mart Platform." In advance of the launch of this great new marketing opportunity, Wal-Mart quietly invites a bunch of companies as well as individual entrepreneurs to get in before they start, so that on launch day they already have an impressive array of prominent participants. A section of Wal-Mart Platform is for causes, but they only invite one presidential campaign to get in early.

On May 25, 2007, that's essentially what happened when Facebook launched Platform, a programming environment that enabled outside developers to build their own applications to run inside Facebook. The Obama campaign was the only presidential campaign to build an app for Platform that was ready for launch day. It allowed Facebook members to see new videos and messages from the campaign and share them with their Facebook friends. Tech staffers from the other presidential campaigns told my colleague Josh Levy and I that they had not heard anything from the company in advance. We speculated that the Obama campaign might have had an advantage because one of its online strategists, Chris Hughes, was also a Facebook co-founder and was still a consultant to the company. But a company spokesman said access to the company's application programming interface had been open to developers prior to Platform's launch, and that the company had "a number of conversations with many campaigns over the intervening months about how they can use the developer API and Facebook Platform."[59] (Farmville and Causes are two examples of such outside apps that have become quite successful from their symbiotic relationship to the social network platform).

The point of this story isn't to accuse anyone of wrongdoing, but more to illustrate the murkiness of the modern digital political arena. In all likelihood, the Obama campaign got in early on Facebook Platform because someone like Chris Hughes was paying close attention to developments in the tech industry and recognized an opportunity to seize a tactical advantage, not because anyone inside Facebook decided to give the Obama campaign the equivalent of an in-kind donation of insider access.

But if Facebook were to tweak its algorithms in some minor way to the advantage of a topic or a candidate, how would we know? If Google were to alter search results in a way that elevated certain information, how would we know?

Google and Facebook are political animals. They have political action committees and have spent tens of millions on lobbyists in Washington and many state capitals in the last few years. Occasionally, as in the fight against the SOPA and PIPA bills, they will use the immense convening power of their platforms and home pages to rally users to take a stand. They also have staffers who are specifically delegated to work closely with both major parties, teaching politicians how to use their tools and hosting a variety of special events and general channels that feature elected officials. To some extent they are a lot like traditional media companies, though they are a lot less transparent about their internal processes: the average news division at a big TV network has much clearer procedures for keeping its operations separate from its corporate parent's lobbying efforts than these tech giants do. Of course, if a platform like Facebook hosts a live town hall-style meeting for a presidential candidate, it risks appearing one-sided. Most corporations avoid taking sides in partisan fights because they don't want to risk alienating half of their customers. But a more subtle kind of king-making might take place and we might never know.

On Election Day 2012, as in 2010 and 2008, Facebook again put "I'm Voting" or "I'm a Voter" buttons on the pages of all its American users above the age of eighteen, 160 million in all.

The company said that it would enable people to click the button, post a story into their friends' timelines, and that users would see the faces of their friends who had already voted along with a real-time counter showing the national total. There were reports of people who did not see those features, or only saw them functioning late in the day. A Facebook source, speaking to my colleague Sarah Lai Stirland, said some users saw different buttons, and others might not have seen the message at all, and that people were randomly selected and placed in control groups as part of ongoing research by Facebook's data team. To date, that research has not been published.[60]

One of the academics involved in that research, Professor Robert Bond of the University of California San Diego, told me recently by email that, "The experiment we conducted in 2012 tests different mechanisms, so we can't say for sure" whether it had the same effect as in 2010, explaining that "While there was definitely still an overall message to encourage turnout, the differences between messages that allow us to estimate their effect was different than in 2010."

He added, "I would expect that the effect of the 2010 manipulation would have been different in 2012 simply because it is a much higher salience election." In other words, we can't assume Facebook's impact on each election was the same because one "manipulation" was in a presidential year, when more people are naturally engaged, and the other wasn't. Also, in 2012, the Obama campaign was highly active on Facebook, which is another new variable. Facebook had also grown exponentially in the intervening years, from 60 million to 160 million adult users in the U.S.

Even still, assuming that the "manipulations" used by Facebook in 2012 had a positive effect on its users' voting behavior, then it is quite likely that Facebook actually tilted the 2012 election towards Obama. That's because the membership and usage of Facebook is not uniform across different demographic groups. According to a major survey by the Pew Internet & American Life Project, women are ten points more likely to use it than men; young people are two to three times more likely to be on Facebook than people over sixty-five; and urban dwellers are more likely to use it than rural folks.[61]

Assuming that the "contagion effect" of the "I Voted" button was uniform, a nudge that increased voter participation by adult American Facebook users probably pushed more Obama voters than Romney voters to go vote, because Obama did better with women, young people, and urban dwellers. Women were 53 percent of the overall vote, and they went for Obama over Romney by 55 to 44 percent. The youngest voters, eighteen to twenty-nine-year-olds, went for Obama by 60 to 37 percent. Big city dwellers gave Obama a whopping 69 percent of their votes; and mid-sized city dwellers gave him 58 percent.[62]

The 2012 election actually wasn't as close as some expected: Florida was the only state where Obama and Romney were separated by less than 1 percent of the vote. But could Facebook have helped Obama win there? In Florida, women were 55 percent of their share of the vote (2 percent more than nationwide); the youngest voters were 16 percent of the vote, a smaller share of their national proportion of 19 percent. If in both cases, the "I Voted" button on Facebook merely caused a .4 increase in turnout across all groups, the verified impact observed in 2010, then due to Facebook's greater popularity among women and young people, it might have increased Obama's total vote modestly, perhaps by twelve or thirteen thousand votes. If the Facebook nudge upped turnout by 2 percent, the high end of the effect found by the *Nature* study, then overall impact might have been to increase Obama's vote by as much as 65,000 votes. He won the state by about 75,000 votes.

When I asked Professor Bond directly if it were possible that the Facebook contagion effect helped increase Obama's vote more than Romney's, he answered, "I would say that it is possible, but that we didn't test for this at all and it would be quite difficult to tell for sure."[63]

Don't Worry, Be Happy

From concerns about privacy and voter manipulation to the power of the private digital platforms where we conduct our online lives, there are all kinds of questions to be asked about where data-driven politics may take us in the years ahead. But the campaign professionals at the top of the field do not seem worried at all. Indeed, as I attended various post-election conferences of political professionals who ran the Democratic and Republican campaigns of 2012, along with outside observers and journalists, it was startling to see how strongly the pros agreed with each other—across party lines—about the wondrous benefits of big data and microtargeting.

"Looking at the left, they've built up a set of institutions and ecosystems built around data and analytics that, quite frankly, I am jealous of," Alex Lundry, the CEO of TargetPoint Consulting, said at the Annenberg School event. During 2012, he was the Romney campaign's data director. He raved about what his colleagues on the other side of the aisle were doing with data:

> They've got Catalist, which does a very good job of being a central data hub, or repository, that is shared across the ecosystem; they've got the New Organizing Institute that is very good at creating a generation of volunteers, operatives and consultants that are data-driven; and the Analyst Institute, which frankly does spectacular work in terms of understanding political motivations, political behavior and political communication, by running randomized controlled experiments.[64]

Another brilliant young Republican consultant, Patrick Ruffini, the webmaster for the 2004 Bush-Cheney campaign who then worked as the Republican National Committee's e-campaign director from 2005 to 2007, wrote that after the 2012 Romney defeat, "The 2012 election should be a wake-up call for those who raise and spend money for the Republican Party," adding that "The election results clearly show that Republican campaigns need to be just as aggressive with their grassroots outreach, online persuasion, and data collection and analysis as their media buys."[65]

Ruffini literally "crashed" the 2012 RootsCamp conference of progressive online organizers in order to learn as much as he could about how the Democrats had so thoroughly beaten his side. He later published a 93-page report called "Inside the Cave: An In-Depth Look at the Digital, Technology, and Analytics Operations of Obama for America"[66] that was drenched in envious admiration for what his rivals had built.

From the central offices of the Republican National Committee to its grass-roots activists, catching up with the Democrats' sophisticated use of data and analytics is seen as critical. In the summer of 2013, the RNC announced a $10 million to $20 million project to build a new technology platform for managing and sharing the party's voter file.[67] And at the annual Right Online conference, the 2013 workshop list looked like it had been cribbed straight from the progressive New Organizing Institute's curriculum. Topics included: "Data hacking 101," "Clicktivism: fighting the battle online," "Tricked out tech: data visualization," "Lean startup: revolutionize your business model," "Mining for treasure: finding interesting data," and "Social and website brand synergy."[68]

The new Big Data practitioners care little for the critiques of outsiders. After hearing various journalists, academics, and privacy advocates at the Annenberg event raise questions about the many ways that campaigns were using voter tracking and data, Rayid Ghani, the chief data scientist for the Obama campaign, even advocated some kind of regulation on such criticism, pushing back against the idea of requiring campaigns to be more transparent about these tactics through some new kind of campaign regulation:

> *So people talk about ethics and privacy from the campaign side, I want to turn it around to people outside the campaign— should there be regulations for them? For them talking about what we do, without any information. Is scaring the public without having any information, should that be regulated? I'm not joking; I'm actually serious. I think the regulation has to come from both sides. There should be some kind of regulation on academics and media when talking about data use by campaigns.*[69]

The odds of any government regulation for how campaigns use data, or of how journalists and academics talk about its use, are close to zero, thanks to the First Amendment. In theory, there might be grounds for requiring more transparency about the use of voter data (in the same way that campaigns are required to make certain campaign finance disclosures), especially since the starting point for this information is public state voter registration records. But the issue isn't going away. Instead, the new technology playing field is quietly warping our pre-Internet understandings of public discourse and personal privacy.

Imagine if when you went to a political rally in a park, the telephone company made a deal with the campaign holding the rally and gave it everyone's cell phone numbers and subscriber information. And then, if you complained about it, imagine that the company said, "Well, you agreed to give up your privacy when you started using the phone you bought from us." Or consider how you would feel if you went browsing for books in a bookstore, and the store monitored which books you took off the shelves, what pages you flipped to, how much time you spent on each book, what you bought, and then made that information available to advertisers and political campaigns. Or what if when you walked into a campaign office to pick up some literature, a hidden scanner took your photo, figured out who you were using facial recognition software, and then somehow got friends of yours already supporting the campaign to contact you later?

These would be chilling scenarios if experienced in old-fashioned "meat-space," but their online equivalents are already happening—and not just thanks to the National Security Agency—especially if we substitute the words "your computer" for "you." When someone uses a computer to visit a website, to browse its pages, or to interact on a social network, all of those moves by that specific computer are tracked by the site owners and their hosting platforms by default. Companies like Facebook have long and confusing "terms of service" notifications that give them the right to collect all of this information, which their users agree to when they sign up for their services. Very few people read these rules, and the companies typically retain the right to change them without notice. Voter-targeting is just a subset of the much larger phenomenon of user-tracking.

Do voters care if data-driven campaigns know so much about their political proclivities? And are they more sensitive to political violations of their privacy as opposed to commercial ones? In July 2012, the Annenberg School released a national survey on public attitudes towards targeted political advertising. On paper, at least, there's no question that voters care. The survey found that 86 percent of Americans do not want "political advertising tailored to your interests." Somewhat smaller majorities also said they don't want ads for products and services (61 percent) or news (56 percent) tailored to their interests.

A supermajority of 85 percent agreed with this statement: "If I found out that Facebook was sending me ads for political candidates based on my profile information that I had set to private, I would be angry." More than three-fourths said they wouldn't return to a website if they knew it was sharing information about them with political advertisers, a much greater percentage than commercial advertisers. Seven in ten said they would be less likely to vote for a candidate if they found out that their campaign was using Facebook to send ads to friends of that person saying they "like" that candidate's Facebook page. And two-thirds said their likelihood of voting for a candidate would decrease if they found out they were tailoring messages to them and their neighbors by purchasing information about their online activities, and then sending them different messages based on what might appeal to each.[70]

Voters may say these practices offend them, but the reality is that all of them are common among today's political campaigns. DSPolitical, a Democratic firm, brags in an online promotion video about taking a campaign's voter file and matching it against the cookies that commercial advertisers have placed in users' browsers, the better to target the right ads at the right people.[71] Targeted Victory, which has worked for Republicans from the Romney campaign on down, openly describes on its blog how it combines voter data with consumer data.[72] All of this is legal. But the super-majorities in the Annenberg poll suggest that though these practices are arguably effective, they may not be wise in the long term.

Some political campaign professionals think there's little to worry about. For example, Jim Walsh and Chris Massicotte, the chief executive officer and chief operating officer of DSPolitical, gave me this statement when I asked for their response to the Annenberg report: "It is understandable that Americans think that they don't want political advertising tailored to them when asked directly. But the simple fact is, and as this report points out, political advertisers have been tailoring messages to Americans since the beginning of the modern political campaign." Or, as Ethan Roeder put it, that ship has sailed.

Walsh and Massicotte even argue that online targeting is less intrusive than older forms:

When cable TV began, political advertisers would choose what channels to advertise on based on their desired demographics and sometimes tailoring different ads on different channels. Tailored online advertising is not very different from tailored direct mail, which has proven very effective. Political Direct Mail firms use the same data that we use to find the right audience for the right message. The only difference is that with targeted online advertising, we don't know where you live, as our ads are targeted using anonymous cookies.

This is a standard response from modern political marketers. And it's true that DSPolitical doesn't specifically target individual people, it just matches their voter data to the cookies that advertisers have placed on those people's computers. The effect is the same. But Walsh and Massicotte aren't worried, because they think their technique is actually good for voters. "Just like any new technology it comes with a level of apprehension," they wrote me, "but once people know more about what it can do, namely spare them from being flooded with useless political ads that they would prefer not to see, more people will accept it."[73] They imply that there must be ads that people would prefer to see, though if that were the case, why would they be ads?

I also received this statement from Rich Masterson, the chairman of Campaign Grid, another Republican firm that specializes in data-driven online advertising, including matching voter file data to Internet cookies. After raising some methodological questions about whether the Annenberg study included only registered voters or included a broader swath of Americans who might be more disaffected by the process, he complained that the researchers "made little to no effort to inform the survey respondents that the technology used for targeting is, in fact anonymous. The presumption that an individual's privacy is violated would lead one to assume the results would be negative." But what the Annenberg researchers found is that Americans don't want ads to pander to their personal interests, whether or not that information was being made available to others.

If Masterson and Campaign Grid are indicative, these tactics will spread, not only because they work for campaigns, but also because the industry thinks it knows what is best for the voter. He closed his reply to me with this riposte:

> *Lastly, there are many surveys that indicate Americans do not like negative campaign advertising, exercise or healthy diets. The fact that Americans do not like these things does not make them bad. Using available technology to improve advertising effectiveness and reduce waste, while protecting consumer privacy, is the new normal for political advertisers. As the market leader in the category we are proud of the work we do and, as the Annenberg survey indicated, clients are embracing the solution for the simple reason that it works.*

There's a big gap between what political practitioners do and what the public is comfortable with. On one hand, the Annenberg study shows that the vast majority of the public doesn't want to feel personally violated, and that political information is of greater personal concern than other kinds of personal information. Political marketers respond that they're not really violating anyone's privacy, because they only use anonymous cookies, never mind that inside their black boxes actual matches between real individual voting data and other personally identifiable information are being made. They also suggest that it doesn't really matter if people say they don't like these techniques: people also say they don't like negative TV ads or direct mail, and those tools have become normal. Why not online political microtargeting?

Maybe. Or perhaps there will be a backlash as more voters ask questions about these techniques. Civic educator Peter Levine of Tufts University writes, "Microtargeting is like using drones: it's great if you're the only one who has them. Of course, it's a lot better to be microtargeted than to be hit with a drone strike, but in both cases, the only decision-maker is the one with the machinery."[74]

With the next American presidential election not that far off, these tensions will only become sharper. The campaign professionals will push for new technological options. Will the public push back?

Here's one glimpse of what is coming from the political drone-makers: at a summit on political innovation that Google hosted in January 2013 at its New York office, top analytics staffers from both the Obama and Romney campaigns had the same essential answer when asked what the hot new tech tool of 2016 would be: "addressable" content, they both said,[75] the ability to send ads directly to individual cable TV subscribers' addresses.

Not to be outdone, a top representative from Google had an equally Orwellian idea. Asked during the summit what was the most effective product the company could offer politics, he answered, "Data analytics plus video on people's phones, so you're right there talking to the person and they can't stop listening to you because you're so interesting."[76] This is not just company self-promotion: according to Eric Schmidt, Google's chairman, YouTube has already displaced TV watching, with more than one billion visitors a month. More American eighteen to thirty-four-year-olds watch it than any cable network.[77]

The day of invisible personalized TV or video advertising that panders precisely to each targeted voter may not be far off. Indeed, in January 2014, Dish Network and DirecTV announced that they were going to start offering this service to political campaigns seeking to reach their 20 million home subscribers.[78] (Political ads will be recorded by your DVR while the TV is idle and then inserted into programming you are watching instead of the commercial ad that was supposed to air.) But today's political data wizards may be living in a bubble, as complacent as the National Security Agency before Edward Snowden's revelations. The press is just starting to show interest in data-driven politics, and all it may take is one courageous whistleblower, or one flagrant breakdown of data security for many more people to start asking if this way of doing business is acceptable.

3

Big Email: The Politics of Passive Democratic Engagement

"Disgusted citizens organize on the Internet:
Urge Congress to Censure and Move On"
—News release, September 22, 1998

We've seen how political campaigns are embracing Big Data, but what does the future hold for advocacy groups? Since the days of Alexis de Toqueville, America has been the land of voluntary associations, where people band together to defend their common interests. In the decades since the 1960s, there has been a veritable explosion in the number of interest groups and trade associations lobbying Congress and the state capitals and trying to influence the public conversation.

The rise of the web and mass participation have altered the playing field for these groups too, but as we shall see, the logic of big numbers, data analytics, and one-sided digital tools have propelled advocacy groups in a direction that is equally worrisome. Welcome to the land of Big Email.

A few months ago I got an email from MoveOn.org, the online Goliath of liberal-left political organizing. Unlike typical emails sent out by the group, which are usually calls to action regarding some current issue, this one is simply titled "How are we doing?" It reads:

Dear MoveOn member,

People have lots of different ideas about what MoveOn.org is, but the answer is actually quite simple: MoveOn is an organization designed to help regular people have a powerful voice in politics.

MoveOn's power and direction come entirely from members like you. The type of work we do together and the issues that we focus on aren't decided by MoveOn's (small) staff, they're decided by MoveOn members.

One of the main ways that happens is using surveys like this one.

Can you take a moment to tell us how you think MoveOn is doing and help set our course together?

The email then provides a link to a web page, the top half of which is shown below.

Can you tell us what you think?

We want to learn more about what campaigns you're most interested in: **Please rank the following by clicking and dragging the campaigns from the left to your list on the right.** You should put the campaign you're most interested in at the top, followed by your second choice and so on. You can include as many as you'd like—**but don't move campaigns on to your list that you think MoveOn shouldn't work on.**

The page offers users a simple way to rank a series of pre-selected issue topics. Below that is a short list of questions, aimed at learning a bit more about what the user thinks of MoveOn ("Compared to a usual week, how well do you think MoveOn is doing this week?"), asking for suggestions, and asking for their attitudes toward President Obama, Democrats, and Republicans in Congress that week. The one-page survey ends with a question: "We always want to be supporting great work President Obama does and encouraging him to do even better. Which of these do you think should be a higher priority right now? Focus on supporting Obama's agenda [or] Focus on shifting Obama's policies to be more progressive."

If you are one of the roughly eight million people currently on MoveOn's list, the odds are that you've gotten some version of this email. Every week, the group asks a few thousand randomly selected members for this kind of feedback. Indeed, the email text doesn't change much; I got a similar email in October 2005 titled "Help us set our course" and the exact same "How are we doing?" email from the group in March 2010. At the time, Ilyse Hogue, then their director of political advocacy and communication, told me the survey responses were "one data point in several that help us make certain we are aligned with our members in any given week."

About 1,000 to 1,500 people typically reply to one of these weekly surveys, according to Daniel Mintz, then the group's campaign director. The staff studies the responses closely. "In the report-back that staff see, we get word clouds based on the open-ended questions," he described. "So if a bunch of people are like, 'We should take on the Federal Reserve,' we'll see it and can then dig down deeper and look at their individual responses. Similarly, if we get a flood of people emailing us about how we should take on the Fed, we'll notice."[1]

In addition to sending these weekly surveys, MoveOn has two additional techniques for listening to its base. The first is fairly old-fashioned: its staff reads all the email it gets from members, whether they are replying to a survey email, a call to action, or just writing of their own volition. The second is essential to all online groups: it A/B tests all of its messages. That is, it tries different options with small samples of its list and pays close attention to how users respond. For example, it might test different subject lines: A: "How are we doing?" vs B: "Tell us what you think." If more people open the first email, then it makes sense to use that subject line.

This methodology comes from the world of direct mail fundraising, but in the online arena it has expanded tremendously for one simple reason. If you have a list of, say, ten thousand or more, or if your website regularly draws traffic at that level, then you can easily segment your audience into smaller chunks and test everything from email language to the size and color of website buttons to see what produces the most clicks. A/B testing was brought to online presidential politics in 2007 by Dan Siroker, a Google engineer who took a leave of absence to volunteer for Obama's first campaign. He taught their team the technique, planting seeds that took root.[2] The Obama 2012 campaign bragged about A/B testing 500 variations on its home page design alone over the course of the campaign, increasing donations by almost 50 percent and sign-ups by 160 percent.[3]

In the United States, MoveOn is the oldest continuously-operating online political mass membership organization. Founded in 1998 by computer software entrepreneurs Wes Boyd and Joan Blades, the group got its start with a petition supporting President Bill Clinton that called on Congress to "Censure and Move On," rather than impeaching him. This petition quickly gathered a half-million signatures. The next year, it created its own political action committee and raised $2 million in online contributions to support congressional candidates, an unprecedented amount.

Then, in 2001, after the 9-11 terrorist attacks, it joined forces with activist Eli Pariser, a twentysomething whose anti-war petition site 9-11peace.org had also struck a nerve. By 2003, the group had more than two million names on its email list. In June of 2003, when it held an online primary asking its members to choose between the Democratic candidates for President, the result was a torrent of donations and publicity for Howard Dean, putting both him and MoveOn solidly on the political map.

Since then, MoveOn has grown steadily, raising and spending hundreds of millions of dollars on behalf of Democratic candidates, much of that on traditional television advertising. It has also inspired, and in some cases actively seeded, a whole network of similar organizations, including the liberal parents activist group MomsRising, started by MoveOn cofounder Joan Blades, which claims more than a million members[4]; the Progressive Change Campaign Committee, co-founded by MoveOn alum Adam Green, which claims about 950,000 members[5]; the African-American online activist group Color of Change, started by MoveOn alum James Rucker, which has about 900,000[6] members; the online feminist group UltraViolet, started by MoveOn alum Nita Chaudhary; the progressive campaign group Rebuild the Dream, co-founded by MoveOn alum Natalie Foster; and the progressive religious online group Faithful America, now run by MoveOn alum Michael Sherrard. MoveOn alumnus Ben Brandzel has been a key driving force behind the founding of an array of international e-groups including Avaaz (which claims nearly

32 million members[7]), LeadNow in Canada, 38 Degrees in the United Kingdom, ActionStation in New Zealand, and Jhatka in India.[8]

The left doesn't have a monopoly on Big Email. FreedomWorks, one of several conservative groups backing the Tea Party movement, claimed 2.1 million members on its email list by the end of 2012.[9] Patriot Voices, the online extension of Rick Santorum's failed presidential bid, claims one million email addresses, as does the online conservative group Grassfire.com. Heritage Action, the grassroots arm of the Heritage Foundation, says it has 400,000 supporters on its email list.[10]

All of them use the same basic model, which is to grow a big list around a common identity, to regularly survey samples of the list to find out what members care about, to A/B test messaging, to monitor results, and to modify messages accordingly. They regularly bombard list members with timely information and calls to action, while also showing list members the collective effect of their individual actions, and raising money to pay for it all by regularly asking for small donations. George Washington University professor David Karpf calls this approach to online organizing—the survey sampling and A/B testing—"passive democratic engagement," though I think the term is apt for the entire model. In his view, this is a major improvement over the way older advocacy organizations involved their members. Writing in his 2012 book, *The MoveOn Effect: The Unexpected Transformation of American Political Advocacy*, Karpf explains:

Driven by a variety of "analytics" tools, MoveOn and similar Internet-mediated issue generalists simply know more about their online supporters than previous organizations could ever hope to. The Sierra Club, by contrast, [where Karpf served for several years as an elected volunteer board member] has historically hired a survey research firm to conduct a biennial membership survey....

MoveOn, by contrast, is capable of measuring, nearly in real-time, which issue topics, message frames, and action requests are of greatest interest to their online membership. A/B testing, in this sense, serves not only to optimize the efficiency of their action requests but also to keep them abreast of member interest.... MoveOn does not need to guess whether a message frame or action is too strident for its membership; it can run a test.... Legacy organizations claim to speak for hundreds of thousands of "armchair activists" who support their day-to-day strategic choices through a small annual donation. By contrast, MoveOn and similar netroots groups are constantly aware of the revealed preferences of their activity-based, online membership.[11]

As interesting as it is to look at how MoveOn listens to and responds to its members, it's also worth noting what the group doesn't do. The last question on the weekly "How are we doing?" survey about President Obama is an obvious way of setting boundaries. MoveOn may be more democratic than the average professional advocacy organization, but it's not going to shift its focus dramatically beyond either supporting Obama's agenda that week or pushing him to be more progressive; certainly not unless its members somehow demand this, en masse.

This reveals a hidden problem with passive democratic engagement: while MoveOn and these other groups actively listen to their members using sophisticated online tools and also devote significant staff resources to this task, they don't enable their members to talk to each other and develop, through doing so, their own sense of what is important for the collective to be doing. Email is a terrible tool for that kind of lateral conversation. The logic of how email works militates in favor of the one-to-many model of communication. The result is powerful and focused, in the sense that MoveOn's members get presented with political action opportunities that "fit" their expressed desires (and admittedly their compressed and busy lives). But the result is also carefully constrained, because it is not the result of an open process. As the Bay Area tech writer Chris Nolan once put it, MoveOn is like "a giant focus group where only the leaders get to stand behind the one-way mirror."[12]

If you have any doubt about where power lies in the land of Big Email, the place to look is obvious: determine who controls the list. The members of these big groups have very little ability to speak to each other at the same scale that the list-owners speak to them. Nor do they have a say in who those people are: none of the groups listed above have leadership elections. During Eli Pariser's time as president of MoveOn, he sent 937,510,800 emails to members in his name, as he notes in his bio. His name became well known. By contrast, if MoveOn mentions a member's name in an email to their list, it is almost always just a first name followed by an initial. Until very recently, there was no foothold for such a person to gain anything close to the standing of someone like Pariser inside MoveOn's mammoth ecosystem.

The Internet's Unfinished Business

Zack Exley was MoveOn's organizing director from 2003 to early 2004, when the group's influence really exploded. Today, his silver hair makes him look older than his forty-four years, but his résumé in online organizing might turn anyone prematurely gray. In 2000, he built a popular parody website called GWBush.com, which led George W. Bush to call him a "garbage man." While working for MoveOn, he took a short leave to advise the Dean campaign. Then he directed Kerry's online communications and organizing, ran the British Labor Party's Internet campaign in 2005, co-founded the New Organizing Institute in 2006, and then went to work for the Wikimedia Foundation, organizing Wikipedia members.

In his view, MoveOn missed a big opportunity to use its massive online list to transform the daily political experience of its members. "MoveOn's business model was its list," he reflected recently. "Let people cry out through a petition, and then fundraise from those people to run traditional campaigns. Its mission was never to create a whole new organization of the people."

The problem, says Exley, was conceptual. MoveOn's leaders didn't know how to use the Internet in a way that would be as productive as their petitions and fundraising. "They couldn't imagine a way that could work where they just opened everything up to their members; they instinctively knew that the worst people would take it all over. They couldn't imagine how to insure that the best people would take it over." And so, when MoveOn asked its members to do something with each other locally, be it a house-party fundraiser or a group visit to the local office of a member of Congress, these events were always conceived as "one-offs" as opposed to launching pads for local MoveOn chapters. Even the few times that MoveOn asked its members to meet up in order to set a larger agenda were conceived as one-time projects, not the seed-beds for regular local meetings.[13]

"One-off events (events that don't repeat) do not shift the locus of political thought and power," says Zephyr Teachout, who was the director of online organizing for the Dean campaign. "It's like the difference between having a local Democratic party club, with functioning committees and purposes, and holding a 'Democratic party office for a day' party."[14]

In early 2003, MoveOn asked its members to organize delegations to lobby their member of Congress against the impending invasion of Iraq. Exley recalls how well that worked:

We sent out an email saying, "we want to lobby every Member of Congress against this war in Iraq," and we need people to play these five roles in each district, and here's the to-do list, and we asked people to apply for these roles. We weren't looking for the most brilliant person, either. All these people applied, and we gave them a checklist. We told them they could improvise, but that these were things they would stick to.[15]

My wife and I went to one of those meetings at the office of Rep. Nita Lowey, who was then our representative in Congress. Thirty MoveOn members from around our district in lower Westchester, New York, met on the street in front of her office in White Plains on a cold February morning. One person had a checklist and signed us all in. Another person asked us to prepare short personal statements, and to try to focus on pressing Lowey to support a delay in the rush to war by letting the United Nations inspectors on the ground in Iraq continue their work of searching for weapons of mass destruction. Another individual acted as the group spokesperson. Everyone, from the aging hippies to the college kids, was dressed in business attire.

The hour-long meeting went well, though many of us were shocked when Lowey insisted that she had no reason to doubt the intelligence reports being touted by the Bush Administration, since the government had no reason to lie. We reminded her that from the Gulf of Tonkin Resolution to the Iran-Contra affair, the government often lied to the American people about its reasons for taking the country into conflict overseas.

After the meeting ended, I was also surprised that none of the volunteer MoveOn organizers made any attempt to collect our contact information. There was no plan to keep our group going as any kind of watchdog or liaison with our representative. Nor was there a sense that we were needed to help MoveOn organize more local rallies or recruit more members.

"I was heartbroken after we got all those groups together for the lobbying and then we didn't let them become an organization," Exley reflected recently, adding that back then he was too junior a member of MoveOn's staff to make a winning argument for a full-scale change in strategy. The local lobbying meetings were unusual for MoveOn because the group's leadership was temporarily willing to let thousands of members do the hard work of organizing themselves. But, he says, the group never again "tried to engage people in a big complex undertaking."[16]

This is not to say that over its fifteen years of existence, MoveOn has never involved its members as co-creators in political action. It has tried a variety of experiments that extended its basic model of aggregating the signatures or donations of thousands of people, offering them other ways to do "one big thing" together. In the spring of 2004, for example, while 2.5 million members strong, it called on members to "Bake Back Democracy" by holding local bake sales to raise funds for its PAC's political ads in support of Democratic presidential candidate John Kerry. More than a thousand events were organized, with names like "Afternoon Tea for Democracy" (in Princeton, New Jersey), "Have Your Cake and Beat Bush II" (in Storrs, Connecticut), and the "No CARB (Cheney, Ashcroft, Rumsfeld, Bush) Bake Sale (in Seattle, Washington).[17] MoveOn's staff plotted all the locations on an interactive online map, and when the sales were over, they collected and displayed a slide show of member-submitted photos.

The bake sales cumulatively raised $750,000 in one weekend, and demonstrated how an organization with a large online membership could solve one of the classic dilemmas of collective action. Normally, most people won't participate in a voluntary political activity because, rationally, they think, "my one vote" or "my one action" can't make a difference. But when people can see that they are part of something larger that has some greater impact, this reticence fades. No one person would go out of their way to hold a bake sale to "bake back democracy," but when large numbers of MoveOn members saw each other stepping forward, the whole project made more sense.

In 2004, MoveOn also broke new ground with its "Bush in 30 Seconds" contest, which invited its members to make their own anti-Bush TV commercial. More than 1,500 ads were submitted and 110,000 people helped sift through them by posting nearly three million ratings of the ones they watched. The winning ad was televised nationwide the week of the Super Bowl, and the contest probably also generated millions of dollars of free publicity. But "Bush in 30 Seconds" wasn't an unblemished success for the group. When the Republican National Committee spotted two user-submitted ads that compared the President to Hitler, it loudly protested, arguing that this proved MoveOn was not part of the political mainstream. In response, MoveOn co-founder Wes Boyd admitted that the ads "were in poor taste" and that the group "deeply regret[ted] that they slipped through our screening process."[18] The experience pointed out the risks inherent in any bottom-up activity, and made MoveOn's leaders wary of losing control of their own brand.

Only in the last few years did MoveOn begin to experiment with inviting its active members to participate in local "MoveOn councils" (and also by opening up some access to its email list, as will be covered in more detail below). Organized through a tab on MoveOn's homepage, these councils are local nodes of progressive activists that hold local rallies, vigils, house parties, and related activities. Their priorities reflect those of the national organization, and MoveOn uses the same kind of analytic tools they use on their website to gauge the interests of council activists. In 2009, MoveOn said these councils organized nearly 5,000 events that were attended by more than 225,000 people.[19] That sounds substantial, but actually it represents a turnout rate of about 4 percent. Had MoveOn started sooner with such local groups, it might have developed a much stronger local network. But as Zack Exley said, it wasn't their business model. In the last year, the councils have been again deemphasized.

In 2007, political scientists Bruce Bimber, Andrew Flanigan, and Cynthia Stohl surveyed MoveOn members, along with the members of two other large organizations, the American Legion and the AARP, for their book *Collective Action in Organizations*. They wanted to find out how often participants in the group had personal interactions with each other, whether face-to-face or online, and to what extent they were engaged in the groups' decision-making activities, either through formal institutional processes or more informal, entrepreneurial methods. What they discovered about MoveOn is illuminating:

> First, like the other organizations, there is a group of members whose interaction is entirely impersonal . . . Moreover, in terms of interaction, MoveOn resembles AARP in some respects: members on the whole rate their interaction with other members as mostly impersonal, although there is also a sizable portion of members who report mildly personal interaction with other members.[20]

Unlike American Legion members, who are much more likely to rate their connections with each other as highly personal, MoveOn members generally don't know each other. But the researchers found that they still feel connected to the organization:

> In spite of the fact that MoveOn is a very large organization composed of members who have no substantial mechanism for meeting one another or interacting face-to-face, members report overwhelmingly that they perceive ample opportunities to guide the goals and priorities of their organization.[21]

The members of giant impersonal online organizations like MoveOn feel like their voices are being heard. In that sense, Big Email works. But while the group's managers can actively poll samples of their membership on a weekly basis, those members have no meaningful way to deliberate together. This is the Achilles Heel of passive democratic engagement. If a new subject arises, there is no forum for internal debate. The councils that now gather a tiny fraction of the group's total membership, and that exist to run local organization campaigns, have no say in the national group's leadership. Nor do these groups have a way to identify weaknesses in overall political strategy or offer pro-active solutions. Like the reactive formations of the networked public sphere, big online groups are best when they are responding to some external crisis or outrage. That makes them well-adapted to our spectacle-driven media system, but not likely to focus much attention on issues when they're not already in the spotlight.

The Revolution Will Not Be A/B Tested

The recent crisis at the end of August 2013 over Syria's use of chemical weapons on its own population, and President Obama's subsequent request for formal congressional approval for retaliatory air strikes, illuminated both these strengths and weaknesses. The Syria crisis wasn't an issue that these groups were formed to address. Nor was there an obvious consensus "progressive" position to promote with respect to this issue, beyond the need to bring the question of armed intervention before Congress. Some members were undoubtedly strong anti-interventionists, wary of green-lighting another American incursion in the Middle East. Others were also worried about genocide, and didn't want to look the other way when mass killings of civilians were taking place.

Therefore, while progressive advocacy groups were much better equipped to move quickly in response to this event compared to their older forbears, Syria wasn't an issue like the crackdown on labor rights in Wisconsin, the Trayvon Martin killing, or the fight for abortion rights in Texas, where the progressive response was clear and all that was necessary to do was to fine-tune calls to action.

The answer to Syria couldn't just be A/B tested. But unfortunately for these online activists, that's the only really good tool in their toolbox. As a result, they either had to admit that their "membership" was divided and confused by the conflicting sides of the issue, or to paper over these divisions with snap surveys.

Take this end-of-August email from Charles Chamberlain, the executive director of Democracy for America, the online continuation of the 2004 Howard Dean campaign, which claims more than one million members:

Subject: What you can do about Syria

To: XXXXXX

I don't need to tell you that the situation in Syria is serious—President Obama's address today made it clear that military action could come any day now. How we handle this as a community is important. Over the last week, I've been hearing opinions, thoughts and ideas from DFA members nationwide. Your feedback has been helpful and informative. Thank you.

Democracy for America is member driven. We respond to your passions. We hear your ideas. We work to understand your goals. And then, as a team, working with you, we provide the leadership to direct our activism as a community into an effective unified voice. But sometimes it's not that simple. This is one of those times.

The email then offered a brief sampling of opinions expressed by DFA members—each of them identified solely by their first name, last initial, and state, explaining that:

Thoughts are still coming in, but after our team reviewed responses from over 40,000 DFA members—including you— only one thing was clear. We are not united as a community. And if we tried to call for one united action in response, we'd be dividing our members—instead of uniting behind them.

So we're going to offer something different than we normally do. Instead of advocating one course of action over another, I want to provide you with the resources to choose your own action based off of the three most common themes repeated throughout the responses.

The email then suggested DFA members call Congress to oppose military force, pointed them to donation pages for humanitarian relief organizations, or prompted them to "put your own idea for action in the hands of our members" by creating a petition on DFA's member-generated petition page.

Or take this September 4, 2013 email from Adam Green, the co-founder of the Progressive Change Campaign Committee (PCCC), which claims more than 950,000 members, titled "What progressives think about Syria." In it he reported that a survey of PCCC members made it clear that they are "anything but undecided" about Syria. "After over 57,000 responses, progressives oppose bombing Syria by 73 percent to 18 percent. That is HUGE."

Green's email added, "Why do folks feel that way? 81 percent believe that an initially-limited bombing campaign would lead to deeper involvement. And 80 percent say, regardless of what our goal is, narrow bombings will NOT achieve it." The email included a link to a memo the group was circulating to members of Congress titled "Your base opposes Syria military action."[22] Interestingly, however, the email also gave PCCC list members the choice to no longer continue getting email on Syria, while promising to continue fighting on the group's other long-standing priorities.

PCCC's numbers seem impressive, but how credible were they? If such large majorities of progressives were fearful of military action, wouldn't there have been more evidence, such as street demonstrations, or social media sharing, indicating a groundswell of opposition?

Unfortunately, the email engagement channel, the main form of interaction these groups have, tends to produce thin results. The fact that close to 900,000 of the PCCC's claimed membership *didn't reply* to the PCCC's Syria poll ought to have made everyone pause. It could be argued that the vast majority of self-identified progressives on the PCCC's list didn't know what to think or do about Syria. The same could have been said of DFA, which only cited responses from 40,000 people out of its one million member list. Such low response rates could be seen as a challenge and an opportunity to develop some deeper ways of engaging those folks that might at least explain why they're not replying. But to raise these questions is to get in the way of Taking Action Now.

MoveOn took a similar path. At the end of August 2013, the group sent out an email titled "Syria" that pushed its recipients to take three steps: educate themselves by watching a video teach-in, to check out the variety of petitions being posted by MoveOn members on their SignOn.org site, and to donate to humanitarian relief groups. Then, on September 3rd, they sent a simple one-question survey to members: "Should MoveOn support or oppose the congressional authorization to use military force in Syria?"[23] The next day, on the heels of Adam Green's PCCC email, came the answer: "The results are in, and they are unequivocal: 73 percent said MoveOn should oppose the congressional Authorization to Use Military Force in Syria." The email from Anna Galland, MoveOn's executive director, went on to cite representative comments from MoveOn members (only identified by first name, initial, and home town), followed by a push to get people to call their representatives.

Galland told me that 109,000 people responded to the survey in the twenty hours that it was open, roughly 1.3 percent of the group's membership.[24] Nevertheless, her email included definitive language about Syria, tying the crisis to MoveOn's long-term identity and mission:

In the early 2000s, MoveOn members helped lead the charge in opposing the misguided U.S. war on Iraq. Now, just over a decade later, the nation again finds itself positioned to enter a war half-way around the world with a country posing no direct threat to our safety or security and with unknowable consequences for years to come.

President Obama is proposing a military strike that raises the specter of another Iraq War—and we're still dealing with the costs of that war today. It's critical that every one of MoveOn's 8 million members pick up their phones today to let Congress know plain and simple: We oppose a military intervention in Syria.[25]

Notably, Galland's language went way beyond anything her email survey asked her members to ratify. It could be that most, or all, MoveOn members, shared this world-view. But nothing in the group's engagement of its members demonstrated that people had reached such a strong, settled opinion.

The real problem with "clicktivism" isn't, as Micah White argued in a 2010 screed in *The Guardian*, that it creates a false sense of efficacy on the part of people who click to sign petitions and so waters down activist energy.[26] It's that it allows the managers of big email lists to think that they are really engaging with a "base," listening to "members" and representing a "community" when actually all they are doing is aggregating the atomized voices of individuals. Faced with the Syria crisis, these groups didn't call for emergency meetings of their local chapters to deliberate about the complexities of the issue. Most of them don't have such things. Nor, in the midst of this sudden crisis, was there time to set them up. Instead, the groups gave individuals a few multiple-choice questions and then did their best to convince mainstream media outlets and members of Congress that there would be huge crowds in the streets if Obama bombed Syria. Luckily, from their point of view, this worked.

Real power isn't just about being able to flood Congress with emails and phone calls—it's also about knitting together networks of people who know each other, understand each other's thinking, and have come to a consensus on how they see the world and how they want to act in it. The managers of groups like MoveOn, DFA, and the PCCC personally participate in such networks with each other, and to some extent with a few of their more dedicated volunteers, but for the most part their so-called members don't even know they belong to anything more than a list.

To be fair, it isn't as if older advocacy organizations that claim to speak on behalf of their membership are any better in these terms. As David Karpf, the author of *The MoveOn Effect*, noted in an email to me about the Syria crisis, "One big lesson here is that the new groups are meaningfully deliberative in a way that the old groups aren't. I've noticed blast messages . . . from 38Degrees, Democracy for America, and MoveOn so far. All adopt a tone of 'this is complicated, we're thinking hard about it, and we'd really like to hear from you.' I've seen nothing from legacy groups. Legacy groups simply aren't wired to ask."

He added, "I think that's fascinating, because it points out *calibration*. Netroots orgs don't ask their members for active direction on every issue. That would be tedious and slow. But they ask their members on the tough ones."

But Karpf also agrees that this isn't enough:

> *On the tough issues, we should craft better deliberative tools than a blast email! I think the big dynamic is that passive democratic feedback should blend into active democratic feedback in times like this. I'm imagining a sliding scale, with different technologies arrayed from passive to active. On one end you have A/B testing—so passive that the members don't even realize the trace opinion data is being gathered. On the other end is a face-to-face deliberative session (online or offline), tied to a binding vote. In between you'd have online membership surveys, yougov online polls, blog comment threads, twitter hashtagged conversations, network backchannel email threads, MoveOn's "member forum," and the Liquid Democracy platform.*

"My perspective is that, ten years in, this is the best we ARE doing, and it's an improvement over the status quo alternative," he concluded.

I disagree. Email may be great for petitions and fundraising around urgent issues where a lot of people agree about something, but the structure of that model is that a few people propose an idea, and then a lot of people join if such a petition or campaign already matches their interest. No one would ever try to use email for a discussion about what to do about a complex issue. Therefore, online organizers tend not to try to involve lots of people in such discussions, and instead try for a proxy effect—a small group standing in for a larger group. The reality is that this isn't really creating much actual power, other than for the people who manage these lists. We are ten years into the process of using the Internet to shift politics, and we should be doing much more.

Worse yet, what these tools and campaigns produce is a weak "we." The members of MoveOn, DFA, or the PCCC haven't really talked with each other and heard arguments that might lead them to change their minds; or even more usefully, understood where the optimal consensus of a large group might be. Instead, the self-appointed leaders of these groups argue that when a majority of a minority of their members take a position, that's a good enough proxy for everyone. Or as Green's email put it, for "the base."

The Rise of the Distributed Campaign

Is there some other way to unleash and coordinate the power of mass participation using email and social media? One method that has come into vogue in recent years is a kind of merger between the energy of free agents and the top-down power of passive democratic engagement that practitioners are calling "distributed campaigns." A number of groups, including MoveOn, have begun to seriously experiment with this approach.

In chemistry, the term "free radical" refers to an atom or molecule that is highly reactive because it contains an unpaired electron and a subsequent dangling bond, meaning that it will often rapidly react with other atoms or molecules. In online organizing, a "free agent" is an individual, or small group of individuals, who are not affiliated with any traditional organization and who use their own organic capacities to mobilize others. Beth Kanter and Allison Fine, the co-authors of the valuable book *The Networked Non-Profit*, have done much to popularize the term. In their view, free agents are "powerful social change players" . . . "who are also fluent in social media and take advantage of the social media toolset to do everything organizations have always done but outside of institutional walls."[27]

Twenty-six-year-old Eddie Geller was just another user of the reddit social link-sharing site in 2010. But the night after the November election returned control of the House of Representatives to the Republican Party, he wasn't willing to listen to his fellow "redditors" grumble about how this was bad news. So he put up a post headlined: "You know what? Fuck this idea that we can't get anything done with a Republican Congress. If we want Net Neutrality (or anything else), then we need to demand it. I propose a Reddit Political Action Committee—not committed to a party or one politician, just good policy."[28]

The next morning, Geller awoke to discover that his post had received hundreds of positive responses. So he created a "subreddit" (a new unique page) for his idea, called it "a place to begin" and said, "May the ideas start flowing." Other users started volunteering their suggestions. One was a lawyer who offered to do the required FEC filing pro bono. Another offered to build a website and database to get the group off the ground and manage its efforts. A month later, Geller had incorporated a new organization, The Open Source Democracy Foundation, gathered a thousand petition signatures in support of net neutrality, and represented other redditors in phone conferences with Federal Communications Commission members.[29]

Geller is a classic Internet free agent, someone whose passion for an issue and facility with social media, plus good timing and a little luck, enabled him to gather thousands of like-minded people around a common cause. It's his existence, and the regular appearance of other similarly successful free agents, that has long tantalized online political organizers, and entrepreneurs with start-ups, who want to do for politics what companies like eBay did to retailing or Amazon to bookstores. They all think that there must be a way to convince millions of disconnected individuals to share their political concerns around a common online hub.

The web is littered with failed attempts at solving this problem, with sites like Voter.com, Vote.com, Speakout.com,

Essembly.com, HotSoup.com, VoteIQ.com, Jumo.com, Votizen. com, and Ruck.us all sinking into obscurity. Indeed, the next time you see a breathless headline about a new website or app that is going to "revolutionize politics," beware. Cumulatively, investors have thrown away tens of millions of dollars on these efforts. It's a genuinely hard problem to solve, since random individuals don't naturally choose to hang out together at any given website. You have to scratch an itch they have and make them want to come back—and do it better than any other competing tools. Reddit itself is actually a pretty good incubator of new projects, some of them political like Eddie Geller's PAC and others even more personally altruistic. But it is also a free-for-all where there is a great deal of exploitative behavior as well.

The closest anyone has come to cracking the code with respect to aggregating online political action is a platform founded in 2007 called Change.org. Its recent innovative approach to online petitioning has led to explosive growth in its user base, attracting more than 50 million worldwide users. In response to Change .org's rise, many other big organizations, including MoveOn, have decided to rethink their whole approach to e-mail campaigns.

I have known Ben Rattray, Change.org's thirty-two-year-old founder, since he first launched the company with a talk at the 2007 Personal Democracy Forum. Painfully, his Powerpoint presentation wouldn't load, so he had to go on stage without the slides illustrating his new site. Back then, he had envisioned Change.org as a one-stop shop where anyone with a cause or issue could easily find the right organization to support. Like Amazon with its huge inventory, Change.org bragged at its launch about having more than a million non-profit organizations on its site. But that was because it had purchased the data. Only a few of those organizations bothered to actually inhabit their Change .org profile page and make an effort to interact with the handful of people who visited. As a result, the site felt like a Potemkin village at first, filled with well-painted storefronts masking the lack of activity inside.

Rattray soon realized that this approach wasn't attracting enough visitors to make Change.org viable. So he decided to shift gears and turned the site from a donation hub into a content hub for causes. Deciding that a better way to find users was through organic search results, he hired editors and bloggers to cover dozens of issue areas like "gay rights" and "global warming." Though creating interesting content around issues did draw eyeballs, it still didn't produce enough engagement. "But then we saw that people were starting to start campaigns and they were winning, campaigns aimed at local targets like mayors," he told me. "So we decided to build the best social action campaign platform possible."

That was in the spring of 2011. At that point, the site had about two million users and was gaining about 300,000 new ones a month. A year later, in 2012, it was six times as big and was growing six times as fast. At that point, Change.org had 37 full-time employees. A year later it was up to 130, and as of the fall of 2013 the company said it had 200 employees in eighteen offices around the world, with more than fifty million registered users.[30]

Why did Change.org take off? The secret to its success was in Rattray's decision to re-engineer the site to be less about content that its editors wanted to highlight, and more about actions that users wanted to take. To be sure, online petitions have been around since the beginning of the Internet. But Change.org is succeeding for the same reasons as YouTube, and it faces some of the same dilemmas as it grows. Before YouTube, it wasn't easy to post a video online, and if that video somehow drew attention, the costs of keeping it online could be painful. The same was true for online petitioning. Plenty of sites gave users the ability to post a petition, but if lots of people started to sign up and you wanted to email them back, you had to pay an email service provider hundreds or even thousands of dollars for every email blast you wanted to send, if this was even possible at all.

On Change.org, not only can anyone can start a petition, the site gives petition creators the ability to keep emailing signers *for free*, along with some smart tie-ins to social sharing platforms like Facebook and Twitter. All through 2010, Change.org's free petition tool was tucked away. However, in late 2010, South African human rights activist Ndumie Funda used Change.org to start a petition to get the government to declare "corrective rape" of lesbians a hate crime. Her fianceé had been gang-raped, and later died as a result. Funda's petition was the fastest growing of any on the site up until that point.

"We would never have started that campaign," Rattray told me. "It would never have occurred to us. And we would never have had legitimacy if we started it."[31] Ultimately, Funda got more than 170,000 signatures on her petition, generating worldwide news coverage. Most importantly, the South African government responded, forming a national task force to finally address the problem. The growth of her petition, and several others like it, convinced Rattray to overhaul Change.org's architecture yet again, de-emphasizing the blogging of issues and making user-generated petitions its centerpiece.

When a petition starts gaining significant traction on the site, Change's staff—which boasts people with deep political organizing experience—jumps in to offer assistance as far as fine-tuning the message, A/B testing email subject lines, and getting press attention. So, while only 1 or 2 percent of the petitions that people launch on the site go anywhere, the law of big numbers is the company's friend. There is an overwhelming number of nascent causes where individuals want action, and by crowdsourcing the early market research, stronger appeals emerge. As Rattray put it during an appearance on *The Daily Show* in April 2012, "We allow a sort of Darwinian process to unfold."[32]

Even if only 1 or 2 percent of the petitions started by site users succeed, with 10,000 to 20,000 new campaigns launching per month, that means there's a steady stream of campaign victories to share with users. And victories, even small ones, are important to keep petition-signers motivated: while Change.org is best known for big campaign wins like twenty-year-old Eagle Scout Zach Wahls' campaign to get the Boy Scouts of America to end their anti-gay policies or twenty-two-year-old nanny Molly

Katchpole's petition demanding that Bank of America rescind a new $5-per-month banking fee, most of the "wins" are of a more small-scale and local character, such as enabling girls to play football in Philadelphia's Catholic Youth League[33] or getting a gym in Bethesda, Maryland to take down an offensive and sexist billboard ad.[34]

Unlike the traditional online petition campaigns that groups like MoveOn have perfected over the last fifteen years, where a small staff uses a variety of tools to decide in advance what issues will cause their members to respond, Change.org flips the funnel[35] and lets its users do all the initial work. Hence the term "distributed campaign." If, in the past, an organization jumped into action in response to some outside stimulus (a crisis or a media event) by crafting a call to arms, A/B testing the messaging, and then driving people to action, in the new model those first steps are distributed widely across the whole universe of people inventing their own calls to action.

Change.org isn't the only platform for this kind of online petition-centered organizing. Around the same time that Change pivoted to its current model, MoveOn launched SignOn.org (now called MoveOn Petitions), which offers its members a similar tool set. In its first year, SignOn generated 18,000 petitions, and MoveOn put the muscle of its big list behind about 600 of them. Steven Biel, SignOn's director, reported. "We've given hundreds of people not just the tools to build a petition, but a network of followers big enough to run a real, ongoing campaign," he says.[36] When someone starts a petition on SignOn, MoveOn gives it a nudge by emailing it to a hundred of its members. If it does well with them, it emails the petition to more people, and so on.

This is MoveOn's most creative response to the criticism that it has been too controlling of its big list. Justin Ruben, who was MoveOn's executive director until the end of 2012, actually called this shift a "bottom-up revolution" when he announced it.[37] But it is not as if the organization has actually ceded all control of its direction to its members. According to Anna Galland, MoveOn's current executive director, the amount of activity generated by the hundreds of petitions in various stages of gestation using the SignOn platform add up to "a full-base email per week," as of the fall of 2013. Something like eight million emails are being sent out each week, but instead of this being one big one from MoveOn staff, it's many smaller ones on lots of different issues. About 30,000 petitions were launched from MoveOn's site in 2013. Even so, the leadership at MoveOn still tries to play a national galvanizing role when relevant:

> We are maintaining some gatekeeper and curating powers at the center of the web here. It's as if we're saying, "Y'all go organize now, do whatever you want to be progressive in your community, but c'mon back because the Tea Party is about to shut down the government, and we have a suggestion of what to do, based on all the things bubbling up among what you are doing locally." It's kind of a swarm model, in distinction to the clashing armies of old.

Galland adds, "From where I sit, what MoveOn is trying to do is catalyze and support and capture where they're happening, these leader-full authentic story-filled moments of emergent campaigning and organizing."[38]

Distributed campaigning is also being adopted by more organizations, especially those with big email lists, thanks to new software from a startup called ControlShift Labs that is easy to integrate with existing systems that organizations already use. So far, the U.S.–based groups 350.org,[39] Credo Action,[40] Democracy for America,[41] and Coworker.org[42] are all offering their members this option, along with Canada's LeadNow, the U.K.'s 38 Degrees, and Australia's GetUp!

According to Murshed Zaheed, the deputy political director of Credo Action, "Distributed organizing takes me back to my own entry into online organizing, when I was helping Howard Dean supporters put together house parties with their own pages on the Dean website. Now instead of organizing lots of parties, we're organizing petitions."[43]

Nathan Woodhull, the coding wiz behind ControlShift Labs, notes that "MoveOn wasn't launched by professionals." His goal is to make online organizing easier for ordinary people to do. "Instead of being the people who decide everything, we're enabling other people to organize themselves," he says.[44] In reality, there's a wide range of organizing that the distributed petitioning approach is enabling. At RootsCamp 2013, Jackie Mahendra, the director of innovation for the Citizen Engagement Lab, a progressive tech hub, offered a four-part taxonomy to distinguish the variety of campaigns that are emerging.

First, Mahendra suggested, there are "wildfire" petition campaigns. Often these are started by people fighting to prevent a friend from being deported or losing their home from foreclosure. Then there are "franchised" campaigns, where a national organization promulgates a tactic, and then lots of groups adopt it locally around a specific target. The current effort by the anti-climate change group 350.org to get universities to divest their holdings in carbon-intensive energy companies is a good example of this. The third type is the "groundswell," a campaign that begins around a local outrage like the Trayvon Martin killing, but then rapidly gains attention and goes national. And finally, there are "hyper-local" campaigns that are typically centered on a specific state, local actors, or timely legislation.[45]

At its best, distributed campaigning has the virtue of lowering the barrier to Big Email, the most effective form of Internet-based political organizing. Giving everyone the ability to send mass emails at zero cost is undoubtedly producing a flowering of hyper-local, local, and mid-level campaigns where victory doesn't require millions of signatures. Sometimes it just takes a few hundred signatures landing in the inbox of a mayor or the manager of a local institution to help tip a battle. For organizations like MoveOn, which still worry about losing control of their brand, the distributed model lets local activists tap their larger list when their petition ideas show merit and allows dumb ideas to die off without harming the larger organization.

These days, fewer people open generic calls to action from big organizations, meaning that a message from a friend or neighbor has a better chance of getting through. In effect, this approach is like the Obama campaign's "targeted sharing," but where petition initiators do all the targeting. In theory, someone who starts a petition on one of these platforms and begins to get a response could easily ask all of her fellow signers to sit down for a face-to-face meeting or even form an organization. Now, MoveOn seems to be saying, if you want to meet your fellow MoveOn members, you can start a petition on a local issue and feel free to conspire with all those who respond.

In at least one case, a very popular petition by a law school graduate named Robert Applebaum to forgive student debt, which garnered more than a million signatures on MoveOn's platform,[46] led him to launch a bona fide nonprofit group called Student Debt Crisis. To Anna Galland, MoveOn's executive director, this is proof that petition campaigns can be "entry points to a larger process of political transformation." She notes that Applebaum has full control of that million-person list he built through his petition.

But there are problems with this model as well. For Change .org, the challenge is most acute because it is a for-profit company, albeit a "benefit-corporation" that says its goal is to maximize change, not returns on investment. Change.org makes money by selling email addresses to paying customers who are typically large advocacy organizations. It places these "sponsored petitions" alongside petitions that are organically

growing, and gently nudges users to sign on. When Change
.org users sign a sponsored petition, a sponsoring organization gets their email address, typically for a dollar or more per
name. And here's the catch: while Change.org started as a portal
for progressive causes, the universe of self-identifying progressives in America probably only numbers around twenty million
people. Additionally, as the company has expanded around the
world, it has become more concerned with offering international
users access to its tools than in trying to determine in advance
whether the causes they are promoting are just ones. To keep
growing, Change.org needed to broaden its appeal, and so in the
fall of 2012 it dropped its "progressive" labeling and announced
it would henceforth be an "open platform" for all causes.

Rapid growth presented a distinct challenge to Change.org's
own business model, one that it was bound to face sooner or later
as its usefulness made it more and more attractive to a wider
range of participants. The company's original client policy said
that it would "accept sponsored campaigns from organizations
fighting for the public good and the common values we hold
dear—fairness, equality, and justice." It included this proviso:
"We do not accept sponsored campaigns from organizations that
consistently violate these values, support discriminatory policies, or seek private corporate benefit that undermines the common good." But over the summer of 2012, Change.org discovered
that this stance was untenable.[47]

What brought matters to a head was the uproar over a
sponsored petition campaign on Change.org by Stand With

Children, an education reform lobbying organization that advocates for more teacher evaluation using student test scores, the elimination of the "last in, first out" seniority system, and other measures that many progressives believe are "anti-union." As David Karpf commented at the time, this presented Change with an unpleasant and perhaps unresolvable dilemma: "They want to be open, they want to promote their own values, and they want to continue growing."[48] According to company insiders, the whole experience brought the company to a standstill for several weeks over the summer as everyone debated the merits of the case and its broader implications.

After extensive internal discussions, Change.org founder and CEO Ben Rattray and his team decided that being open should be their paramount value, rather than trying to decide whether each and every advertiser they take is a true-blue progressive. Company spokesman Benjamin Joffe-Walt said:

> *Our strategy is to create a global empowerment platform that is open to anyone, anywhere and that helps democratize access to power for hundreds of millions more people. We want to help build a world where no one is powerless and making change is a part of everyday life. And we think we can do that best through empowering people everywhere to make the change they want to see. We think the net positive impact on the world will be greater if we're an open platform than if we're an agenda-driven organization, even if that openness means that some*

people many of us personally disagree with are able to launch campaigns on our site.

As part of this shift, the company published new advertising guidelines that no longer talk about "fairness, equality, and justice" and instead describe its goal as "empowering people everywhere to create the change they want to see." The guidelines say that Change.org will not accept ads from hate groups, or ads that promote hate, violence, or discrimination, and that it reserves the right to refuse advertising "based on technical limitations, resource constraints, or protection of the Company and our users." This made sense for a company that was growing and trying to be a big platform for change. As a leaked internal planning document pointed out, "closed guidelines [for potential advertisers] . . . simply don't scale." It would take too much time to research every individual advertiser, and doing so would also imply that the company was endorsing the advertisers whose causes they did accept. "Ultimately, we need to get out of the business of making subjective judgments about advertisers or having public battles about the ads on the site, which distract our team from the important work we're doing," the document argued.[49] For Change.org the company, this was the necessary move to make, but for much of its original user base, it was a betrayal.

The essential difference between Change.org and MoveOn/ SignOn is largely one of economics. In order to sustain itself, Change.org needs advertisers and sponsors who pay for access to live email addresses. So it has to take more of a mass, "neutral" approach to its market. MoveOn/SignOn pays for itself by asking its users for donations. As long as they identify with its values, it doesn't have to water anything down. If Change.org is *The Washington Post*, then MoveOn/SignOn is National Public Radio.

Welcome to Spamalot

A second, larger problem that afflicts the whole world of Big Email and passive democratic engagement is, paradoxically, the by-product of email's continued popularity. That is, compared to other web-based engagement tools, email is still the "killer-app," the cheapest way to raise money online and spur action. As a result, we all get too much of it and we're responding to less of it, whether we are ordinary civilians or the politicians and other entities who are the targets of online petitions. So while all of these groups keep trying to optimize the responsiveness of their lists and fine-tune their social media tactics to make their content "go viral," they are avoiding addressing a systemic problem with their strategy: their targets' and supporters' attention spans are finite. The more emails they send; the more email sign-ups they need to have an impact. The more everyone uses social media, the less any but the biggest groups can focus our attention.

In 2004, Congress reported receiving more than 200 million communications, 182 million of which came via the Internet.[50] Over the course of the decade, the Congressional Management Foundation found that congressional offices experienced anywhere from a doubling to a tenfold increase in the amount of communications they receive from the public. On just one extraordinary day, January 18, 2012, it is estimated that anywhere between 10 and 20 million people emailed, called, and/or faxed Congress to express their opinion on the then-pending SOPA and PIPA bills. "Every year it gets more difficult to keep up with the level of correspondence that comes into the office," one House legislative director told the foundation. "It's over-whelming and it seems like we can never do enough to keep up with it."[51]

Most members of Congress and their staffs say they ignore emails or other social media messages from non-constituents, and pay little attention to all electronic communications they receive, whether from constituents or not. Letters, phone calls, and office visits matter much more. And yet, according to a 2012 study by Shayna Englin and Stefan Hankin that explored the gap between what advocacy organizations do and how Congress responds, a whopping 95 percent of the activists they surveyed from eight major organizations said they had signed an online petition and 91 percent said they had sent an email directly to an elected official. Less than half said they had called an elected official, and less than a third had ever attended an in-person meeting with one.[52]

When you lower the cost of making something, more of it will be produced. But digital communication by email and social media is so cheap that we are making far too much of it. Internet analyst and author Clay Shirky calls this a tragedy of the commons. Says Shirky: "Instead of producing signal for representatives about the strong feelings of their constituents, we're now in a PR battle for which campaign has generated the most email. It's like the McDonald's business model: billions and billions of emails served."[53] And the rarely spoken truth is the digital arms race to build a bigger list or get more likes and shares is unwinnable.

This hasn't stopped the advocacy industry. Longtime digital campaign strategist Jake Brewer calls this the "tragedy of advocacy." In 2010, Brewer wrote:

Many . . . advocacy groups have become incredibly savvy at enticing us to "share" or "act" with Congress online, employing professional staff that do nothing but try to get us involved. I know because I've been one of them for years. Ultimately about 82 percent of all citizen action in the United States is generated through these teams at third-party organizations such as the AARP, Greenpeace, or Focus on the Family, producing anywhere from 300 to 2,000 email messages delivered to each Congressional office every day—not to mention the barrage of Tweets, Facebook posts, and other messages.

Unfortunately, the very technology that has allowed virtually any citizen to share a message with their representative has also produced paralyzing noise, making Congress far less able to hear what citizens have to say. The modern Tragedy of Advocacy is that all this increased share-your-voice-i-ness of citizens with Congress has actually resulted in more reliance on specialists and less on constituents than ever before. Congressional staffs often need those specialists (typically the dreaded "lobbyists" we love to hate) simply to distinguish signal from noise.[54]

In the past, a petition campaign that got 500,000 signatures, like MoveOn's first "Censure and MoveOn" anti-impeachment call, was seen as a big deal. Now it takes a million or more signatures to get the mainstream media to really stop and take note. Likewise, when the Obama administration launched its "We the People" petition portal, it took just 5,000 signers to trigger an official response. That hurdle has since been raised twice, first to 25,000 and then to 100,000.

But making the hurdle for attention higher just keeps the arms race going, a contest where inevitably the only way to get more eyeballs or clicks is to make your message more sensational, more spectacular, and more emotionally transfixing. That is, more manipulative.

The same problem is apparent in the parallel competition for online traffic among digital news publishers. For the Huffington Post, which started as an aggregator of original blog posts by a mix of celebrities and serious newsmakers, this has meant adding sections to its website like "Sideboob" and featuring reports on a "Man Sentenced for Public Sex With Pool Toy"[55] on its "HuffPostLive" video news channel. For BuzzFeed, another fast-growing site, it has meant converting nearly every story it publishes into some version of "19 Times The 'Spongebob' Writers Said Screw Logic."[56] And for Upworthy, a fast-growing social sharing upstart co-founded by MoveOn's Eli Pariser in the spring of 2012, it means teasing online readers with "clickbait"— headlines that have been A/B tested to perfection to get people to click on a piece of content by hinting at but not quite telling them what they will find. Upworthy got 87 million visitors during the month of November 2013,[57] making it a new cultural force. However, it remains to be seen how making the Internet's version of Casey Kasem's Top Forty List is supposed to lead to real political change, which is Upworthy's stated purpose.

Companies like Change.org and Upworthy make money by selling email addresses to other organizations hungry for fresh names, at roughly a dollar or so per name. At the micro-level this is innocuous. Good Cause Organization wants to grow its email list; it has money; it spends that money most efficiently by paying for fresh email addresses from Change.org or Upworthy. Assuming that the people whose addresses are being sold are opting in to being on Good Cause Organization's list, everyone is happy.

But at the macro-level this starts to look like a plantation system for farming money and attention from ordinary people. Now, instead of building its own family farm network for growing supporters, Good Cause Organization obtains them by buying them wholesale from the big plantations. After all, these big plantations have developed scientific techniques (like A/B testing and writing twenty-five headlines per piece of content) that vastly improve old-fashioned yields. And where do all those Good Cause Organizations get the money to pay the plantations for their fresh crops? At least in part by emailing their own list to ask for money.

Upworthy is also moving in the direction of producing or hosting "sponsored content," developing a greater emphasis on topics like labor, parenting, or global health which are of interest to potential sponsors like the Gates Foundation.[58] In this and other ways, Upworthy is starting to look a lot like a TV channel or radio station. Its content aggregators are the producers. They find talent, make sure it's ready for prime-time, and then someone else on staff tries to match that up with sponsors. Upworthy headlines are like pointers to really great short TV shows. In essence, the company is saying to netizens, "Don't watch TV, watch this instead." On the one hand, this shifts power away from traditional commercial TV. On the other hand, it's still a lot like TV in that the main thing it asks its users to do is to watch something. Could it be that the epitome of successful political web organizing is to reproduce the old one-to-many broadcast model?

Shirky has a radical alternative. "First," he says, "raise the cost of communicating. When the cost of communicating falls too low, the signal falls with it." Then, he adds, "Design for groups, not just aggregates. One way to raise the cost of communicating is to get people who come together around an issue to do something other than just fill in their name, a zip code, and click. Get the people who support your cause to do something to support your cause." And third, he argues, "Regard elected representatives as partners, not targets. From their point of view an email campaign is basically spam."

He admits this is like asking nearly every advocacy organization to abandon the core of its current model of public engagement:

> It means stepping out of the current arms race, almost unilaterally disarming in this competition for bigger and bigger lists and button clickers. If we don't do that, there's a risk that digital activism will continue to run down the path it is heading, away from civic engagement and towards crowdsourced PR. If I had to take those changes and bundle them up in one sentence, what I would most want to see in terms of rethinking representation is more effort into helping groups send real signal rather than continuing to engage in competition for increasingly meaningless political noise.[59]

There's no question that a substantial new infrastructure of organizations and networks has been built on the left, and to some extent also on the right, since the beginning of the 21st century. Some of these groups are pure digital natives; others are hybrids that have combined old-fashioned brick-and-mortar facilities with new online capacities. The numbers on the left alone, like the numbers generated by the 2012 Obama campaign, are quite impressive, especially if we include companies like Upworthy and Change.org that are much more mainstream in their approach:

> Upworthy's visitor total for November 2013: 87 million[60]
> Change.org's user base: 50 million[61]

Avaaz's email list (includes international): 31.9 million[62]
Organizing for America's email list: 30 million[63]
Care2's email list: 23.5 million[64]
MoveOn's email list: 8 million[65]
Planned Parenthood's email list: 7 million
Credo Mobile's email list: 3.4 million[66]
SumOfUs's email list: 2.2 million[67]
MomsRising's email list: more than a million members[68]
Progressive Change Campaign Committee's email list: 950,000[69]
Color of Change's email list: 900,000[70]

But beyond successfully electing and re-electing a man named Barack Hussein Obama, nearly all of online advocacy's greatest victories lie far from Washington, DC, in the realm of cultural politics or in direct pressure on corporations. Campaigns targeting advertisers directly have been especially effective: Presente .org's campaign to get Lou Dobbs taken off CNN worked especially well after activists got people in Latin America, where the network is expanding, to join in; UltraViolet's targeting of advertisers on Rush Limbaugh's radio program in the wake of his sexist comments about feminist activist Sandra Fluke cost him dearly; and Color of Change's "Stop Glenn Beck" campaign ultimately won after many advertisers pulled their dollars from his show.

In addition, online organizing has had several successes by going after powerful corporations. For example, as I mentioned earlier, Molly Katchpole's wildfire campaign on Change.org shamed Bank of America into dropping a proposed $5 monthly surcharge on its customers after 300,000 people added their voices. She then turned her sights on Verizon's addition of a $2 fee for online bill payment and after more than 130,000 petition signatures, the company backed down in less than twenty-four hours. And after the killing of Trayvon Martin sensitized many white Americans to the perverse logic of "stand your ground" laws, activists turned their sights on the American Legislative Exchange Council, a shadowy lobby group that helps corporations develop legislation for state legislators. More than fifty corporations have since dropped their membership in the group, costing it millions of dollars.

But why haven't all these groups with their big lists, savvy targeting, and nimble ability to capitalize on breaking news managed to make a bigger impact on national politics itself? The netroots has helped elect several Senators, like Elizabeth Warren, Jim Webb, and Jon Tester, along with a handful of Representatives. But just as many of its champions have lost their congressional bids. And why has there been so little traction around more structural issues that shape the game of politics, like campaign finance reform or proportional representation?

Big Email campaigning conceals several weaknesses. First, because of the hyper-noisy media environment, today's online campaigns work best with emotional triggers. A campaign in response to an outrage like a Trayvon Martin killing or a bank gouging its customers is far more likely to gain traction than a campaign to pass a bill to end "stand your ground" laws or toughen bank regulations. Outrage against something is easy;

organizing for something takes time. It's the "stop/go" problem. The KONY 2012 movement's near-total collapse just weeks after its video reached tens of millions of people shows just how hard it is to convert momentary passion into lasting power when you are reliant on today's online infrastructure.

The second weakness is just as hard to address. While there may be something like 20 million Americans who go online and sympathize with progressive values and causes, it's only a slight exaggeration to say that there are nearly as many groups seeking their attention. The 2012 annual convention of Netroots Nation was illustrative. Wandering the convention hall in Minneapolis that weekend, I spotted sessions on cultural organizing and youth, building on the Wisconsin labor fight, forcing action on "don't ask don't tell" and the DREAM Act, dealing with "wage thiefs" who steal workers' earnings, decoding monetary policy, organizing around community colleges, environmental justice, protecting reproductive rights, combating corporate power in elections after the Citizens United ruling, fighting against dirty energy industries, "working the refs," and fighting for marriage equality. There's a wonderful kaleidoscope of efforts underway to fight the good fight, and while I salute the good intentions and hard work of the people involved in these causes, the Internet has both made it easier for them to pursue their individual passions and harder for them to come together for something larger.

Many weak causes do not add up to a stronger movement. Daniel Cantor, the founding executive director of New York's Working Families Party once tried to make this argument in the days before the Internet. Noting how many small groups managed to just keep themselves afloat with costly direct mail campaigns and annual fundraising dinners, he told me he wished he could convince people to give more money to fewer groups, to force some consolidation of forces, especially towards groups doing multi-issue community organizing. The right, he noted, has the ability to use big money to corral people into larger efforts; the left doesn't have the same ability to incentivize better behavior. Without that kind of leverage, today's Internet-powered activists may be fated to stay disunited.

Lastly, as Shirky and Brewer both point out, there's something hollow about the way that so much online organizing gets converted into action—not only are fewer people clicking on each email they receive, most recipients of those emails in Congress discount their value. That is not yet the case for petition campaigns aimed at local officials or corporations, but there's good reason to fear that those targets, too, will start to question whether they should really care about such missives if they don't come from actual constituents or customers.

Paradoxically, the public's embrace of social media may well be making it even harder for most advocacy organizations to get attention to their issue. A recent academic study looked at 257 transnational human-rights groups and their efforts, from 2010 through 2012, to generate media attention in both traditional outlets as well as on new social media platforms like Facebook, YouTube and Twitter. Its findings are sobering. The biggest and best-funded groups, like Amnesty International, Human Rights

Watch and Oxfam, got half of all the mainstream media coverage. Twenty-six organizations—just 10 percent of the entire group studied—received 91 percent of all the news coverage, as well as the lion's share of Twitter followers, Facebook likes and Youtube views. The organizations with annual budgets of over $100 million a year were the biggest winners in both media categories.

According to the study's authors, social media didn't help level the playing field at all for the smaller groups, though even the poorest ones, with budgets of less than $1 million a year, used social media nearly as much as the richest groups. "The least visible 50 percent of the [non-governmental organizations] in each medium are in fact getting as much attention as the average *individual* user of Facebook or Twitter," they wrote.[71] That is, even though these less well-known organizations were trying to develop a following online, now they were competing for attention with a much bigger universe of content-creators: all of the individuals using Facebook and Twitter themselves! The fundamental problem is that there is only a limited amount of attention that can be paid by an audience to what is happening in the world. Increasing the number of people speaking and sharing content doesn't lead, in the aggregrate, to more attention to that content, it leads to greater fragmentation.

What is to be done? Is there an alternative to a politics shaped by Big Data and Big Email? First, we need to insist on tools and platforms that genuinely empower users to be full citizens. And second, we have to take back our own digital agency. We have to insist on more control of our own data, and more disclosure of how other organizations, ranging from the government and political campaigns to commercial enterprises, track and use data about us. If necessary, we may have to creatively disrupt the smooth workings of that data-gathering system by taking more direct steps to restore our privacy. Nothing less than our own ability to be full participants in the decisions that affect our lives is at stake.

4

The Way We Look to Us All

"Only connect! That was the whole of her sermon.
Only connect the prose and the passion, and both will be
exalted, and human love will be seen at its height. Live in
fragments no longer. Only connect, and the beast and the
monk, robbed of the isolation that is life to either, will die."
—E.M. Forster, *Howards End*

The Internet does not have to become one more means for mass marketing and manipulation. It can also transform civic life into something far more participatory, transparent, and engaging. And rather than just work as a tool for petitioning and protest that a few people use on behalf of much larger atomized groups of individuals, it can link problem-spotters with problem-solvers, and make everyday life better in myriad ways.

As Ami Dar, the founder of Idealist.org, a hub for listing volunteer service opportunities, likes to say, "Our problems are connected, but we are not."[1] That is, most people don't know who lives near them, or what they may be thinking about important issues. The way Big Data now works, only the managers of giant data-streams have a comprehensive understanding of who is interested in what. For example, Google knows who is searching for terms that relate to the flu, and can use that information to build a model that predicts where outbreaks are taking place. It can even (and does) serve up useful medical advice for such search results. But if lots of people are getting the flu somewhere because their city has inadequate health services or high unemployment, they have no way of addressing the larger pattern behind these individual complaints, nor does Google make this common interest visible to the people it concerns. Likewise, MoveOn may know that a substantial chunk of its membership wants the group to take on a new issue, but those members have no way of knowing that unless MoveOn's staff chooses to tell them. Important data flows upward, not sideways.

The rise of the Internet as a political platform is also a very mixed blessing for anyone who believes that public discourse thrives best in public places, given how few of the places where most people converse online are actually public. On the one hand, networked media make a different kind of public possible, something the digital media scholar Dave Parry calls "the Internet public." Those of us who devote at least part of our time to being laterally connected with other people via new media are developing a different expectation about our role in society, one where we can be more active participants in creating and shaping news and culture. Channeling media theorist Marshall McLuhan, Parry argues that the medium through which we communicate changes social relations between people and thus changes the society we live in.

For example, Parry says, if the Komen Foundation had changed its policy on funding Planned Parenthood breast-cancer screening ten years ago, before the rise of the Internet public, little would have happened. Now, anger gets expressed visibly, socially, publicly, and instantly in ways that can have a political impact. And when the Egyptian government shut down the Internet at the height of the "January 25" protests during the Arab Spring, that action had the effect of pushing more people out into the streets, helping to accelerate Hosni Mubarak's downfall. Parry writes, "While the Egyptian government could mostly shut off access to the public Internet, they couldn't shut off the Internet public. That is, while the government could shut down the hardware of the Internet, it could not shut down the social effects of the digital network."[2]

However, generally speaking, the Internet public hangs out in the digital equivalent of privately controlled shopping malls, not public squares. And the problem isn't just that most of the "places" we use aren't local, the way that a genuine town hall meeting or neighborhood forum brings together people from the same district or community; it's also that corporate portals mostly function as vertical siloes for the like-minded. When a politician holds an online town hall meeting on Facebook or Google Hangout, that choice not only privileges people who have high-speed broadband access, which is just half the U.S. population, it also leaves out anyone who doesn't want to create a

Facebook or Google Plus account. We are a generation into the Networked Age, and our public infrastructure of schools, libraries, parks, and government institutions, all places where "we the people" can congregate in the flesh, have not been replicated online.

"Though we are not lost, we are losing," Sue Gardner declared at the 2013 MIT-Knight Civic Media conference in Cambridge. From 2006 to 2013 Gardner was the executive director of the Wikimedia Foundation, which publishes Wikipedia. Taking the long view on the evolution of civic media since the rise of the Internet, she said, "We certainly have no information-sharing participatory Garden of Eden, the promise of the Internet that we all originally believed in."[3] Other than Wikipedia, which is the only nonprofit website in the top twenty-five most visited worldwide, the web is dominated by the platforms and values of for-profit companies, where the average person spends most of their time.

On Wikipedia, participation is transparent. No one is required to register in order to make an edit on a page, but the site remembers what IP address an edit came from. That's how we know when edits to the pages for Congress get made by people working inside Congress: there's one IP address for everyone working in the Senate and just a few for the House. It's easy to view the history of edits on a page, the traffic statistics to each page, even the number of people who are watching a particular page. And you can look up the history of any user's edits: Sue Gardner's Wikipedia edits on everything from Chelsea

Manning's page to the "country of origin effect" are easily spotted.[4] In other words, user behavior on Wikipedia is as public as people congregating in a park.

By contrast, participation on platforms like Facebook or LinkedIn is hidden. And not just by Facebook users who choose to keep most of their posting private; Facebook keeps all kinds of user data to itself. You can't find out who has looked at your Facebook page; at LinkedIn you can determine this if you are willing to pay a premium price. You may be a subject of interest, but the platform gets that data, not you. If you post something to these sites, the platform decides where it gets pushed, and again, it will charge you for the privilege of reaching all of your friends or followers. If you had your own website, you would know much more about who was visiting your page and you would have much more control on how your information gets shared.

Participation on Facebook is also shaped dramatically by the ubiquitous "like" button. There's no way to "dislike" anything on Facebook, something that advertisers certainly appreciate. But imagine going to a real-life town hall meeting where the only way to comment on something was first to "like" it. Developers are literally banned by Facebook from making a "dislike" button for people to use, and they also aren't allowed to make apps that might encourage people to "unfriend" each other.

In protest, Dean Terry, the director of the emerging-media program at the University of Texas at Dallas (and a former colleague of Dave Parry's), and Bradley Griffith, a graduate student, created EnemyGraph. The tool, which Facebook users added as a plug-in to their accounts, allowed them to list people or things that are their "enemies."[5] It worked for a while, and then it broke when Facebook made changes to its software architecture.

The single most valuable piece of civic software anyone has made in the last ten years is also a piece of public property. I'm speaking of the lowly hashtag (the # symbol), which has enabled all kinds of movements to focus their communications, ranging from Iran's 2010 election protest (#iranelection), Egypt's #Jan25 revolution, Tunisia's #sidibouzid revolution, #OccupyWallStreet, and even #TCOT (top conservatives on Twitter). Far beyond politics, all kinds of public community conversations are loosely knitted together by common hashtag. And it's the property of no one, not Twitter the company, nor anyone else. It was just the inspired idea of an early Twitter user, Chris Messina, a web developer who borrowed the syntax from its use to identify Internet Relay Chat channels.

On August 27, 2007, Messina tweeted, "how do you feel about using # (pound) for groups. As in #barcamp [msg]?"[6] His purpose, he said then, was "in simply having a better eavesdropping experience on Twitter," which was still in its infancy. More seriously, he also wrote that he wanted to improve "contextualization, content filtering and exploratory serendipity within Twitter."[7] He kept pushing the idea, and then a few months later was gratified to see usage of the protocol take off during a spate of wildfires in California, when people started tweeting with "#sandiegofire" about the news. Photos on the picture-sharing service Flickr were also being tagged the same way. "Hashtags are far from perfect," he wrote then. "I have no illusions about this." But he thought sharing emergency information around the San Diego fires was a great use case for the larger problem he was hoping to solve, which was to "coordinat[e] ad-hoc groupings and giv[e] people a way to organize their communication."[8] Little did he know how successful hashtags would be.

When he was asked years later why he didn't patent the idea, Messina answered, "claiming a government-granted monopoly on the use of hashtags would have likely inhibited their adoption, which was the antithesis of what I was hoping for, which was broad-based adoption and support—across networks and mediums." He added: "I had no interest in making money (directly) off hashtags. They are born of the Internet, and should be owned by no one. The value and satisfaction I derive from seeing my funny little hack used as widely as it is today is valuable enough for me to be relieved that I had the foresight not to try to lock down this stupidly simple but effective idea."[9]

"The web started indie," says Tantek Celik, a longtime coder and "alpha geek" who now works for Mozilla, one of the only other major organizations like Wikipedia that is devoted to developing the public infrastructure of cyberspace. By that he means that the early sites on the web were mostly put up by independents (scientists, academics, and bloggers), and the first wave of tools like HTTP, email, and RSS were not owned by anyone but were simply useful sharing systems that benefited everyone.

But now in the age of Facebook, YouTube, and so on, Celik says, "If you post your content to these sites, you're basically giving up your rights."[10] In his spare time, he is one of the driving forces behind IndieWebCamp.com, a community focused on reviving and growing the independent web, where people control their own sites and data. The IndieWebCamp site jokingly quotes the character Morpheus from the movie *The Matrix*: "You're here because you know something. What you know you can't explain, but you feel it. You've felt it your entire life, that there's something wrong with the world [wide web]."

Why do we need the "Indie Web"? Celik's site offers a long list of reasons[11]:

- You're afraid of losing your photos and files (some users of Apple's MobileMe service lost theirs when Apple moved to the iCloud service in 2012).
- You're frustrated by downtime (services like Twitter, Flickr, Tumblr and even Facebook and Google have all suffered glitches).
- Your account was frozen (people get booted off Twitter for tweeting too much,[12] or from Facebook for all kinds of obscure and often-unexplained reasons[13]).
- Your account access was removed because you were using a pseudonym (as happened to Egyptian democracy activist Wael Ghonim, who lost access to his "We are All Khaled Said" page just as the anti-government demonstrations in Egypt were cresting in 2011[14]).

- Your blog was deleted for obscure reasons (Google blocked adult content from Blogger, its blogging service, without explaining what defined "adult"[15]).
- A post of yours was removed because of legal threats that you didn't have a chance to know about or respond to (this often happens with complaints under the Digital Millennium Copyright Act[16]).
- Your blog was disappeared because of dubious trademark claims (as happened to danah boyd's Tumblr blog[17]).
- Your identity is misrepresented with no avenue to correct false information (as happened to writer Amy Wilentz when Google decided she was dead[18]).
- Your content was taken and its ownership transferred without permission to a big copyright holder (as happened to one YouTube user who uploaded a video of himself foraging in the forest and discovered his video was removed because the birds chirping in the background supposedly matched a music video licensed by Rumblefish, a music content provider[19]).
- You don't want a platform taking your content without your permission or payment (as Instagram attempted to do at the beginning of 2013[20]).
- You don't want your content used to advertise things that you never agreed to advertise (which Facebook recently gave itself the power to do).

The last reason is perhaps the biggest one: "You're done with sharecropping your content, your identity, your self." The original sharecroppers were people who were allowed to live on agricultural land in exchange for giving the landlord a share of the crops they produced. Often they barely eked out a subsistence living. Today, people who post their content on platforms like Facebook, LinkedIn, Google, YouTube, and the like are all being digitally sharecropped. As the saying goes, "If you're not paying for it, you're the product." The real customers are advertisers and other people who want to make money from our data.

The larger point is that architecture is politics,[21] and coders are legislators.[22] Every choice the designers of a website or platform make about the way their service interacts with users contains subtle, implicit decisions about power. The fact, for example, that the Uber taxi service doesn't enable its drivers to laterally communicate with each other is critical; the owners of Uber don't want to make it easy for drivers to organize with each other. "The insiders are winning," Wikipedia's Sue Gardner warned in her MIT speech.[23] For the health of society, she argues, we need a flowering ecosystem made up of the digital equivalent of public parks, libraries, and schools where people can connect to each other on free terms, not just one Wikipedia as the exception to the rule.[24] But the most obvious answer to this problem—that government, which was the seedbed for the development of the Internet—should look for ways to ensure that some part of cyberspace is open to all, is nowhere on the current agenda. And this is truly odd, given how democracies have treated public space for decades.

"If the government said that people can't drive on the roads to go to a rally in a public park to protest something, because it would lead to bad press, everyone would protest," comments Tom Steinberg, the founding and guiding force behind the United Kingdom's MySociety.com, the first civic hacking collective. "Yet when government says that it can't let people using government websites to connect to each other in order to challenge the status quo, no one says anything."[25]

In Steinberg's view, which I share, a .gov website should include features for citizens to create their own online presence. After all, if the local library can give you a library card, and the state can give you a driver's license, why not give people the option of owning their own online presence through a public platform where the data they make is theirs to control? Such a system could make it easy for people with similar concerns to connect laterally, creating needed competition with today's siloed advocacy organizations. And it could shield their interactions from the predations of commercial and political marketers. Among the many challenges we face in reclaiming democracy in the age of the Internet, one of the hardest is creating genuine public spaces for interchange.

Additionally, if people are to have any greater ability to participate in the decisions that affect our lives, then we need to be able to see what our data collectively says about us. We need to know "the way we look to us all," as songwriter Paul Simon put it, in as fine and flexible a way as our would-be Big Data overlords seek to know us.[26] (Recall how much the Dean for America blog enabled tens of thousands of Dean supporters to create a collective self-awareness, and how little the Obama 2012 campaign did.) We also need to be engaged with our own data in practical ways that enrich us, not just the technocrats using it for their own purposes. To turn the so-called "Smart Cities" movement on its head, we need to make sure connection technology helps us become smarter citizens, and doesn't just make our cities better at managing us.[27]

Unfortunately, the digital tools we rely on most heavily were not built with these goals in mind. Most critically, none of the services we all commonly use for digital communication—email lists, blogs, chat, and wikis—were designed for group decision-making. In *Here Comes Everybody*, Clay Shirky's seminal book, he wrote that we were living in an age of "ridiculously easy group formation." But what he left out is that starting a group is not the end of the story. Keeping a group organized and functioning in a way that makes its members want to stay involved is hard. It's no wonder that most online political groups in America are built around having common beliefs rather than working on solving common problems. That's because the communication tools we use are great for self-expression and terrible for reaching consensus, particularly when there is disagreement. Think of how most of us use the digital tool-box:

- Email list-servs may be great for letting everyone have the opportunity to speak, and they may be useful for sharing basic information among members of a group. But any attempt to make a decision using a list-serv is bound to consume hours of everyone's time and risks creating confusion, and, almost inevitably, flame-wars.

- A top-down email list, by contrast, doesn't really give its members the ability to make decisions together: at best, the list's owners may do regular surveys of membership opinion; at worst, they do A/B testing to optimize the response rate on a choice that list members have little or no say in generating.

- A blog, either written by an individual or a group of contributors, may be a great way for a few people to project their vision and rally a community. But blogs aren't designed to be democratic decision-making tools. Invariably, they are the vehicle of their authors.

- A chat room (like Internet Relay Chat) might work for a small group of intimates who are used to working with each other, but chat doesn't scale well, either for groups of people who know each other or strangers. The same is true for Facebook chat threads or your run-of-the-mill Twitter conversation around a common hashtag.

- Wikis can be great places for groups to share ideas in common, and they even allow everyone to contribute on an equal playing field. They are the closest thing we have to group collaboration platforms. But many people find wikis hard to edit, except for the hard-working nerds who keep many wikis going. Consider the process Wikipedia went through when its American branch "decided" to go dark to protest the pending SOPA/PIPA bills. The "Jimbo Wales talk page" that acted as the village square for the community discussion on this proposed action gathered roughly 2,000 individual comments and stretched across roughly 50 screen-scrolls.[28] If you had tried to print it out the scroll would have been at least 25 feet long. When a group needs to make a decision, no one says, "Let's use a wiki to hammer out how we feel."

- Finally, there are the many specialized tools that groups may use to help with handling complex tasks, ranging from free ones like the meeting scheduler WhenIsGood.com, to cheap ones like Meetup.com, to sophisticated (and somewhat more expensive) collaboration platforms like Basecamp and Campfire, built by the company 37Signals. They're nifty and helpful, but they're basically project management tools, not group decision-making tools.

The good news is that it is possible to make the Internet and Big Data work for democracy. Online community hubs focused on solving real-life problems are not only already here, in some places they're hitting critical mass and changing the culture of the places they serve. Group decision-making tools that can enable hundreds of people to deliberate together, even when separated by space and time, are spreading. And a new crop of digital innovators are developing a variety of promising ways to open up Big Data to all of us. The future impact of the Internet on politics may well be different than the one now being charted.

Creating Citizens Out of Residents

To see how the Internet can change civic life in deep and positive ways, there is no better example than SeeClickFix. com, a community platform that was founded in 2008 by Ben Berkowitz, a computer programmer living in New Haven, Connecticut, with the help of his friends Miles and Kam Lasater, and Jeff Blasius.

They started the site after Berkowitz, then twenty-eight years old, tried to report some unsightly graffiti on a neighbor's building. After calling the New Haven city government, nothing happened. "I got the idea that my neighbors were reporting similar things, but there was no accountability and no collaborative discussion," he recalled later.[29] So he and Kam Lasater hit upon the idea of creating a website where anyone could post a problem that needed fixing on a public map, and then the site would email the report to the addresses of top city officials. They reasoned that making the reports transparent would make it harder for city hall to ignore them, and easier for community members to rally around the most urgent issues.

At the time, Robert Smuts was New Haven's chief administrator, a position which made him effectively second-in-command to the mayor. He told me that the city had launched a similar input channel on its own website, but it didn't get much use. "Instead, we started getting flooded by these emails from SeeClickFix," he recalled with a chuckle. "The service we had gone with was designed by government. SeeClickFix was more user-driven, more driven by the resident public." He admits that there was "some grousing" inside city government about all those complaining emails, but as he says, "SeeClickFix didn't create the pothole, it just made it easier for people to report it." In response, he started integrating SeeClickFix's reports into the city's internal management system.

Six years later, SeeClickFix has become, in Smuts' words, "the universal front end for the city of New Haven, for non-emergency reporting." Indeed, not only is a link to SeeClickFix featured prominently on the top right corner of the city's official website, the daily flow of fresh reports from residents is also posted on the online front pages of the city's two main newspapers. In New Haven, Smuts says, about ten thousand reports flow through the system each year, half from public SeeClickFix users, and half from city employees taking a report from a member of the public by phone and inputting it directly into the SeeClickFix site from their desk.[30] The city pays SeeClickFix for access to an internal dashboard that helps to manage the flow.

About 170 cities across America have similar relationships with SeeClickFix, including Albany, Albuquerque, Atlantic City, Houston, Minneapolis, Oakland, Raleigh, Washington, DC, and Winston-Salem. The states of Massachusetts and Utah are also customers. Berkowitz says about 350,000 registered users have signed up, and more than 670,000 issues have been reported and resolved across all of those sites. The company, a privately-held for-profit that makes money by charging cities for its service, is growing steadily.

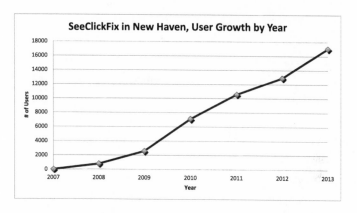

SeeClickFix in New Haven, User Growth by Year

In New Haven, 17,000 people have SeeClickFix accounts, about 12 percent of the city's population. It has taken Berkowitz and his colleagues six years to reach that level of usage. Along the way, they have made a variety of important design decisions aimed at maximizing SeeClickFix's potential to become a central community hub for problem solving. For example, when a problem report is marked resolved, which the responsible city agency representative usually does, any resident can re-open the issue. "What's most important is not that city hall thinks something is solved, but the citizen has to be happy," Berkowitz told me.[31] That's a design decision that, politically, situates ultimate power in the hands of the users, not the clients, of SeeClickFix. They've also added a "Say Thanks" button that encourages users to acknowledge when a problem is resolved; each Friday the site then sends the person who was responsible for fixing that problem an email with the names of all the people who thanked them. And if someone chooses to follow a specific problem or location, the software will automatically alert them to "points of interest" within a five-block radius of the issue.

Users can earn "civic points" for a variety of actions such as commenting on an issue (5 points) reporting an issue (10 points), getting an issue you reported closed and archived (30 points), getting at least one user to comment, vote, or follow your issue (50 points), creating a watch area (50 points), and logging in seven days in a row (100 points). The more points you get, the more impressive your title. Users with 250–500 are listed as "civic crusaders"; those with 1,000–2,000 are "digital superheroes"; and those with more than 10,000 get the "Jane Jacobs" label in honor of the famous urbanist. As people learn the ins-and-outs of getting things fixed in their town, they can contribute to a do-it-yourself "frequently asked questions" wiki that is designed to help everyone, include city staffers, know the right answers to these questions.

If architecture is politics, then Berkowitz and his colleagues have designed SeeClickFix to maximize visible connections and activity between neighbors. The result is a kind of "thick" civic engagement between ordinary residents, elected representatives, and city officials that merges the online and offline worlds and, in the best of cases, is helping cities like New Haven do something more important than just save money or respond more quickly to residents' complaints: it is growing social capital.

Berkowitz calls potholes "the gateway drug to civic engagement" and says he looks forward to spring, because it's the time of year when the warming weather reveals all the streets in need of repair after winter in the Northeast. "This is my favorite time of year," he wrote on his blog in March of 2013. "It separates accountable from unaccountable governments in a tight time frame with simple anecdotal evidence that government is working or not. More importantly late winter is a time where citizens are engaging passionately about block level concerns. This also presents a great opportunity for those looking to engage with citizens on a deeper level than potholes." He added:

> At SeeClickFix we like to capture frustrated citizens, harness that frustration and point it towards engagement with feedback loops created by neighbors and governments. This Spring will bring lots of new users who come to the platform to vent. In the following months they will likely engage with other content that helps build a better more citizen driven neighborhood, help a neighbor find a lost pet or actually resolve an issue with their own hands. We've been optimizing this algorithm for neighborhood engagement for the past 5 years and every year it gets more interesting as the outliers on the platform become more common place and repeated across communities. Bring on the potholes, good governance and great citizenship.[32]

Here's an example of SeeClickFix in action. On August 29, 2013, a dog was abandoned behind a building on Audobon Street in downtown New Haven. Part pit bull and part boxer, it was tied up and in distress. Someone going by the user-name MableX (with 880 civic points) took a picture with her mobile phone and posted a brief report on the site. "Animal Control does not answer the phone and the police said to call animal Control," MableX wrote. "Mailbox of Animal Control officer filled so I called my Alderman to see if he could help. Went looking for police officer on Whitney, none to be found."

Within minutes, another SeeClickFix user, Robbin (with 195 civic points), responded, "I am available if someone needs to come stay with the dog until animal control responds . . . I live on Chapel St. and can be there quickly."

Soon after that, the city alderman for that district, Doug Hausladen (with 26,925 civic points), chimed in on the thread: "Robbin—please do! He needs some water—I got the call from the constituent but i'm tied up at work. I also forwarded to animal control and left messages (as did the constituent). keep me posted if anything changes," he added, posting his cell phone number.

Robbin replied, "On my way . . . with water & I'll grab some dog biscuits."

Then a police officer named Sgt. Means, using a guest account, posted: "Spoke to the supervisor at animal control. Complaint received."

Meanwhile, MableX was still paying attention to the conversation, even though she couldn't stay with the dog. "Thank you for looking into the safety of this dog. Someone from ACES got him/her a blanket and bowl of water. Found out dog belongs to a homeless man. Hope this is not a 'Mr. Bojangles' scenario."

Robbin soon popped up again. "I am with dog . . . female . . . i brought food . . . she was hungry . . . very tame dog but definitely happy for attention, food & water . . . will wait for animal control . . ."

And then, about an hour after her first report, MableX marked the issue closed. "Animal Control Officer came and retrieved dog. Thanks to ACES and Robbin of Chapel Street for tending dog," she wrote. Then follows some idle repartee amongst several users on whether this episode mirrored the dog in the song "Mr. Bojangles," along with about fifteen other people chiming in to simply say, "Thanks for fixing this issue."

That wasn't the end of the story, however. A little more than a week later, a guest user of SeeClickFix named Christina reported seeing the same dog again tied up and abandoned. And three days after that, another guest user questioned whether getting the dog to Animal Control was such a good idea, writing "do you honestly think any time in that cold, blanketless, heartless, shelter will be anything but torturous?" Someone else agreed, and marked the case "reopened."

That was followed by posts from several guest users, all speculating about conditions in the animal shelter. None of them were happy about the dog's prospects. And then, amazingly, Officer Stephani Johnson, New Haven's Municipal Animal Control Officer, chimed in with a lengthy guest post setting the record straight.

"If you would like to visit OUR shelter you will see that 95 percent of our adoptable animals are Pitbulls or Pit part mixes awaiting new homes, not being euthanized as they walk in the door just because of their breed," she told the doubters. Further defending her agency's work, she wrote:

Are we understaffed, YES, but we work hard caring for our animals, feeding, cleaning, triage and daily care of sick animals as well as assisting the public with complaints, introducing animals to potential adopters, school tours, food assistance and referrals for rehoming pets, just to name a few. We do not have a receptionist so we must answer the phone and return all calls when time allows. We do not close for lunch as similar agencies do and our breaks are when we can get them. We make every attempt to address everyone's complaint, issue or concern.

Then she asked for help placing animals for adoption and asked for donations of food and supplies. "You can walk in my shoes for a day," she told the shelter's uninformed critics, listing specific opportunities for volunteering. And then she closed out her post with the facts about the dog that started the whole thread:

Now here's the update. . . . . . . Five-Year-Old "Lady", who is in great shape, was reclaimed by her owner the following day. He gave a physical address but we believe he is homeless. "Lady" was picked up again a week later when she was found tied behind another location. He sent a friend in to confirm she was at the shelter and asked that we find her a home. She is a happy dog and it is quite evident that her owner loved her as she shows it in her temperament. She will soon be placed for adoption and maybe DC [the original critic who questioned the shelter's work] can recommend a new family for her. Thank you all for being patient, caring and assisting.

After that, two more guest users left comments. One said, "We all appreciate the work that people like you do for the four footed citizens of this country. I suggest that those who are most critical of shelters get involved in one locally and offer their time to help alleviate the burden of the workers or contribute in other ways. Just complaining is not helping." And the second one railed against the divisive tone that the skeptics brought to the conversation, saying, "Let's try to work together on an issue we clearly all care about rather than against one another." To end things, MableX—the original passerby who started the thread by reporting the abandoned dog—closed the report again, and begged everyone to have more of a "wee bit of humor" about life in New Haven. And then, some icing on the cake: another guest user also thanked Johnson for her comments, adding, "I am about to take my first step toward volunteering at a shelter. Baby steps for me, a little at a time . . . Thank you for sharing, Stephanie. It paints a much better picture in my mind of what to expect."[33]

Stop and consider what took place on this single thread (which had been viewed nearly 2,000 times, by the time of this writing). First, a concerned passerby spotted and reported a public problem. A neighbor heard about it and decided to take action.

The elected representative for that local district also responded, nudging the responsible agencies in city government while also supporting the citizen taking action. A local cop reported that help is on the way. The representative and the Good Samaritan both kept everyone informed on the situation, and then the original passerby, still monitoring the news from afar, declared the problem solved. All of this happened in real-time on a website that anyone could use.

Then, a concerned but skeptical resident asked for accountability, fearing that the service provided by the city was sub-par. Other residents, citing rumors, fueled that worry. And then, the responsible city official responded with her side of the story, using her real name and giving plenty of checkable facts. Two residents offered support, and the issue got closed again, transparently. And then the open discussion had the effect of inspiring at least one new person to volunteer her time to civic improvement.

Half a decade ago, before SeeClickFix existed, this scenario would likely have unfolded this way: someone would have called 911 or Animal Control to get the dog. The dog would have waited alone until their arrival. The alderman would probably have called the police for help, but then he would likely have moved on to other business. And would anyone have felt any sense of urgency? The shelter might have taken the dog in, but would its staff have been scrutinized with respect to how they cared for it? Would any of the local residents have seen each other getting involved, or known of the responsiveness of their city agencies and representatives? And finally, would there have been an easily accessible record of the entire encounter, including contact information for various involved parties or the number of times they had been civically active? To that final question, we know the answer: absolutely not.

"There's a lot of dialogue between city staff and members of the public," says New Haven chief administrator Robert Smuts. "A lot of it starts off snippy and exasperated," he notes. "There are always trolls out there, but it pretty quickly evolves into an appreciation of the work being done and the effort being made." He adds, "It's also interesting to see the public organize itself around issues—either to get the city to address something, or to address it themselves."[34] Paul Wessel, a former city director of traffic and parking, another longtime community organizer, says, "It's an integrator, a connector. It functions, in some ways, like a faster, better, letters-to-the-editor page, but one that has the ability to connect to a work order system."[35]

"We all have heard the stories of entire neighborhoods that sat idly by while a person screamed for help," Ben Berkowitz reflected later on his blog, ruminating on this one abandoned dog incident. "It is awesome to know that the community that I get to work with every day is not that community."[36] The woman who went to help the dog, whose full name is Robbin Siepold, told me by email that she had heard about its situation from a SeeClickFix email alert. The site lets users subscribe to alerts for specific areas, and she used to work for a company in that part of downtown. She explained what happened next:

Having been laid off from that company, I was home that day—I live downtown on Chapel Street across from The Green, and hence my ability to jump into action quickly. I have a passion to help animals in need, so there was no hesitation on my part to help out.[37]

For Alderman Doug Hausladen, SeeClickFix is more than just a bulletin board where anyone can report a non-emergency issue of public concern. "What SeeClickFix actually does is it's creating citizens out of residents," he told me at a coffee shop not far from where the dog was reported abandoned.[38]

Not only that, the site also makes it easy for community groups to form around bigger local issues than potholes and abandoned dogs in order to channel public discussion in productive directions. The New Haven Safe Streets Coalition, for example, has used SeeClickFix to post more than 3,000 issue reports.[39] "I remember posting red-light runners all over town, back in the day," Hausladen says, recalling his years as a community activist working on that issue. "We'd have little SeeClickFix stakeouts. It's a very open, transparent way of documenting an issue. We'd create watch areas, and then follow search terms like 'red-light runner' as well."[40]

In 2010, Hausladen was part of a coalition of local community groups and activists who used SeeClickFix to try to address another serious local problem: food deserts. The Shaw's supermarket had closed, leaving a hole in downtown services. Hausladen posted a call to arms on SeeClickFix, urging people to help "Bring back a full-service supermarket to New Haven" and asking them to take an online survey cataloging their concerns, the better to lobby public officials and potential entrepreneurs on this demonstrated need. The post was a major hub of conversation in town about the problem, with nearly 200 comments and more than 12,000 views.[41] It took close to a year, but ultimately the city and community convinced a Stop-and-Shop to occupy the vacant property.

The existence of SeeClickFix hasn't solved all of New Haven's problems, of course. Like many cities in America, it is economically and racially divided. When Mark Abraham of Data Haven mapped seven years of crime incident reports alongside all the SeeClickFix service requests, he found that the densest areas of SeeClickFix usage were in the safer, more upper-middle-class parts of the city (though SeeClickFix reports do come from every part of the city). Crime reports, unsurprisingly, were concentrated in the poorer neighborhoods. To Abraham, this indicated that in less well-off areas, not only were residents less likely to use digital media, they also had greater reasons not to trust government to come to their aid.[42]

Having roughly one in eight New Haven residents as registered users of SeeClickFix means that local life works differently. Berkowitz told me of a recent case where he had observed a thief break into a parked car and make off with someone's bags. He called the police, but he also posted a SeeClickFix report, in the hope that someone might alert the car's owner. The thief had left the car window open, and it was starting to rain.

"In a previous reality, the only way to find that person is to go into nearby businesses and ask if someone knows whose car that was, which I did do," Berkowitz reflected.

In a previous reality.

He notes that he could have tried calling out to people via a Facebook post or tweet, but neither of those services really have the "geo-specificity" he needed. His post showed up on the local newspapers' homepages, and probably even more importantly, it sent emails to anyone who had had issues near that location on SeeClickFix. It turns out that the car's owner was the guest of someone living on the street who was indeed a SeeClickFix user.[43]

"This is something that could have only been created by the Internet," Berkowitz mused. "In essence, we've created a community APB [all-points-bulletin] for non-emergencies, that works on everything from lost animals to car break-ins. You can drop a needle in a haystack, and now it's easier to find it, because the haystack is better organized. This is a fundamental shift in the way we think about neighborhoods."

SeeClickFix's success in places like New Haven represents the leading edge of a new political synthesis that is just starting to emerge in America, something akin to the "neutral point of view" balancing act that has enabled millions of people to contribute to Wikipedia despite their many differences. It is a new form of collaboration that uses technology, open data, and public participation to solve shared problems. It isn't "e-government," where the authorities use the web to provide information and services, but "we government" sustained by peer-to-peer connections around the issues and needs that matter most to people. "We government" could be our path out of the small government vs. big government debate.

But self-reinforcing civic engagement takes time to build. Few people know that better than Steven Clift, who founded E-Democracy.org in 1994 and has been building local online neighborhood forums in Minneapolis-St. Paul for nearly as long. Discussing the subject recently in a Facebook chat with me, he said, "If you have an online commons where ideas can be spread, you have to have the patience for things to spread and gel." In his view, tech-enabled local change can help hasten neighbor-to-neighbor connections, but they still don't crystallize quickly.

"Here is a real live example—an effort to improve ski trails at our local public urban golf course was proposed online in 2011," Clift wrote. "Dozens responded and then they organized." Two years later, they won a $1,000 "Big Idea" challenge in a local participatory budgeting contest, he reported, and they also started petitioning the city for better service.[44] "This all happened in local democracy/community because people connected in the 'common' local interest could have a near friction-less two-way conversation and find each other on an emergent issue," said Clift. "You sort of see this on Twitter on global and national happenings on a very temporary basis with more opinions than action or Facebook Pages/Groups after some big disaster . . . but this tends not to scale down well locally outside of disasters or hot (often protest) moments EXCEPT in my view where communities have local-up online public spaces in their neighborhood or community."

He explained:

> For those of us who want a big global spread of this civic connecting, our lack of a "neutral" and trusted directory that allows for national/global marketing of where you can connect (and a corresponding massive outreach and promotional campaign) online like this is a huge barrier. The reality is that most people who haven't experienced this do not search for local common interest connecting spaces online—unless they are moving from a neighborhood where they have experienced this and expect that every neighborhood must have this—so we need a network or network promotional effort (and definitely not just one platform).[45]

That day has yet to come, but thick online-empowered local civic engagement is on the rise. A Burlington, Vermont start-up called Front Porch Forum began in 2000 when a couple who had newly moved to the city decided to reach out to their immediate neighbors and invite them to join a small local email list. It took them six years, but eventually 90 percent of their neighborhood had joined. At that point co-founder Michael Wood-Lewis decided to quit his day job and set to work spreading the model across the county. Each forum is limited to about 400 homes, so the conversation, which is moderated by a community volunteer, stays civil and focused on local concerns. The idea proved popular and so they founded more groups, each covering a little more of the city. By 2010, two-thirds of Burlington's residents were in a Front Porch Forum group.[46]

In the small town of Moretown, Front Porch Forum was a godsend when Tropical Storm Irene hit. In the year beforehand, says Wood-Lewis, "book clubs were formed, dog-walking groups got together, the school's PTA got stronger, more people were showing up for events. So when a disaster hit, it wasn't a bunch of kind of vaguely familiar strangers who weren't sure how to reach each other. They were living in a community."[47]

And in the wake of the storm, which devastated the state in August 2011, the company started to expand. By February 2013, it had 47,000 active members across 90 Vermont towns, and in September it announced plans to expand to cover the whole state. New members are signing up at the rate of hundreds a week, Wood-Lewis says.[48]

Not every local online platform will succeed like SeeClickFix or Front Porch Forum, however. In both cases, careful curation of the community conversation has been essential. Outside.in, a more data-driven local social network site, was bought by AOL and disappeared from view inside the local news network Patch, which itself has also been drastically downsized. Everyblock, a different kind of local news site that aggregated open government data along with public streams to show people everything from Flickr photos to restaurant health ratings near them, faced a similar fate when it was acquired by MSNBC.com, which was then bought by NBC News. A year later, Everyblock was shut down because it wasn't profitable enough.[49] Those challenges haven't stopped investors from pouring more than $40 million into NextDoor .com, a start-up that was founded in 2011 and describes itself as a "private social network for you, your neighbors, and your community." It now claims to be serving more than 25,000 neighborhoods across America; in my home town just thirty people out of nearly 8,000 residents are members, and the growth rate is a feeble two or three per month.[50]

Reimagining Leadership and Decision-Making

In the same way that the Internet can transform how local life works at the neighborhood and city levels, it can also change how entire groups organize themselves and make decisions together. But while the Internet's architecture is open and horizontal, most of us grow up in settings that are inherently hierarchic. In the family, parents rule over children; in school, administrators and teachers rule over students; in the workplace, bosses and managers rule over workers; in traditional religious organizations, priests, rabbis and imams rule over worshipers. The same is largely true for politics, where campaigns as well as governmental offices are structured for hierarchic command-and-control. Ingrained in all of these institutions is the expectation that one person, the leader, will make decisions for the rest of us, and our job is to know our place.

Democracy, if it exists at all inside any of these entities, is usually understood as majority rule. The winner takes all. Most of us get little chance to participate in the decisions that affect us, other than by voting once every two years. Inside the organizations where we spend most of our daily lives, the same situation is often true. Voting with dollars—that is, being choosy consumers—is for many people the only form of direct representation that they have.

For some advocacy organizations, the solution to this problem is representative democracy. Take the Sierra Club, which has 2.1 million members. Many of its decisions are actually made first by groups, then by chapters, then by the national board (composed of people elected by chapters) that go to the executive director who then enforces those decisions. This process has the effect of empowering members, but it can be slow and constricting as well. The organization doesn't have as nimble an online program because of other priorities set forth by this democratic process.

The Sierra Club model, which political scientists refer to as a federated association, used to be the rule across America. For a long period from the Civil War through the 1950s, national, mass-membership associations with local, regional, and state elected leaderships and regular assemblies, dominated civic life. As political scientist Theda Skocpol documented in her invaluable book, *Diminished Democracy: From Membership to Management in American Civic Life*, some two dozen organizations—including the AFL-CIO, the National Congress of Parents and Teachers (PTA), the Free Masons, the American Legion, the Young Men's Christian Association, and the American Farm Bureau—had anywhere from 1 to 12 percent of the population each as members, as late as 1955.[51]

For decades, millions of Americans learned how to participate in public life through membership in these organizations, many of which brought together people (mostly men) across class lines. Skocpol cites an article from 1892 in *Century Magazine* that purported to explain to a foreigner how it was that America could be such a sprawling, open, and yet stable democracy when in fact only a few positions of high political distinction were available to office-seekers: "Here then we have the great American safety-valve—we are a nation of presidents."[52] That is, there were so many branches and chapters of these mass-membership groups that hundreds of thousands of people could be elected to positions of standing. Indeed, according to Skocpol, in 1925, somewhere between 3 and 5 percent of the population had served in a leadership position in a civic organization.

This has all changed in the last fifty years, for a variety of reasons that are beyond the scope of this book. Suffice it to say that, per Skocpol, federated, mass-membership cross-class organizations were undermined by cultural conflicts fostered by the Vietnam War and the struggle for civil rights, along with the rise of suburbia and the spread of broadcast media. These groups were replaced by a proliferating array of professionally run, top-down advocacy organizations heavy with lawyers and lobbyists, like the AARP and Natural Resources Defense Council, with a much different structure and kind of interaction with the general public. "America is now full of civic entrepreneurs who are constantly looking upward for potential angels, shmoozing with the wealthy," rather than talking to people of modest means, Skocpol once said.[53]

Writing in 2003, this is the civic landscape she saw:

> The very model of civic effectiveness has, in short, been upended since the 1960s. No longer do civic entrepreneurs think of constructing vast federations and recruiting interactive citizen-members. When a new cause (or tactic) arises, activists envisage opening a national office and managing association building as well as national projects from the center. Contemporary organization-building techniques encourage citizen groups (just like trade and professional associations) to concentrate their efforts in efficiently managed headquarters located close to the federal government and the national media. Even a group aiming to speak for large numbers of Americans does not absolutely need "members" in any meaningful sense of the word.[54]

The Internet, and the culture it makes possible, is different. It has no center or leader. Rather, it is at heart a set of shared principles for how computers should inter-connect, hammered out over time and practice by an open network of computer engineers who make decisions "by rough consensus and running code."

Proposals are circulated as "requests for comment" or RFCs. According to Stephen Crocker, a computer engineer who wrote the first RFC, "Less important than the content of those first documents was that they were available free of charge and anyone could write one." He adds, "Everyone was welcome to propose ideas, and if enough people liked it and used it, the design became a standard."[55]

This way of operating can seem alien to people brought up to expect hierarchy the same way they breathe air. In *The Starfish and the Spider*, Ori Brafman and Rod Beckstrom's seminal book on the power of leaderless organizations, there is a delightful story about the first "President of the Internet." Dave Garrison, the CEO of an early Internet service provider named Netcom, was in Paris, trying to raise money from a group of investors at a fancy hotel restaurant. "One of the investors started asking who was the president of the Internet," Garrison recalled:

> *We went in circles about how "there is no president." . . . It was very funny. But this is 1995, early '95, so the Internet is still an unknown thing. We're explaining, "It's a network of networks" [. . . and] "There are thirty to forty thousand networks, and they all share in the burden of communication." And they said, "But who decides?" And we said, "No one decides. It's a standard that people subscribe to. No one decides." And they kept coming back, saying "You don't understand the question, it must be lost in translation, who is the president of the Internet?"*

Finally, Garrison says he gave in and said he was the Internet's president. As Brafman and Beckstrom write "If we're used to seeing the world through a centralized lens, decentralized organizations don't make much sense."[56]

I suspect this is why so many people had difficulty relating to Occupy Wall Street when it emerged back in 2011. Two months after the movement burst into view with the first takeover of Zuccotti Park in downtown Manhattan, *The New York Times'* Public Editor Arthur Brisbane wrote a column titled, "Who is Occupy Wall Street?" Though he quoted a reader who told him that the movement's lack of traditional leaders was an essential part of its message, he couldn't let go of the idea that it must have some. "An investigation into [its] origins would lead to the identities of early leaders, at least, and the search for the broader leadership of the movement should continue from there," he wrote.

A sampling of leading journalism educators that Brisbane polled, many of them former top newspaper editors, agreed. "Most said it was important to understand who the leaders were and what demographics they represented," Brisbane reported. "Leadership tells you a lot about a movement," Jerry Ceppos, the former executive editor of the *San Jose Mercury News*, told Brisbane. "But I can't cite the name of a single Occupy Wall Street leader. I know some members say the groups are 'leaderless.' But I have trouble believing that this is an entirely organic movement that grew without a leader. I'd push hard to see if there are leaders and to profile them."[57]

The insistence on finding the supposed leaders of Occupy Wall Street came from more than a desire to understand the movement's goals. For many traditional political observers like Brisbane and his colleagues, the notion that a political movement might arise without charismatic leaders was inconceivable. Every previous movement, after all, has had its figureheads. Think of Mahatma Gandhi, Martin Luther King, Nelson Mandela, or Lech Walesa. The same question was raised around the Arab Spring uprisings in Tunisia and Egypt, which were also often described as "leaderless."

In fact, political movements can't be leaderless. The Occupy Wall Street movement was, like the uprisings of the Arab Spring, full of leaders. The people who started it wanted to avoid the traditional top-down leadership where most participants leave decisions to the people on the stage. They chose instead to rely on a face-to-face "general assembly" model of consensus-driven decision making. Their preference for peer-to-peer networks and working groups created space for lots of leaders to emerge, but only ones that worked as network weavers rather than charismatic bosses. Willie Osterweil, one of the participants in the summer conversations in New York City that led to Occupy's emergence, put it this way in a private email thread from early August 2011, which he gave me permission to quote:

We don't want observers, we want participants. We don't want to convince someone in an elevator ride to sign a paper or donate money, we want people to express themselves and experience and fight for freedom. We don't want a media headline, we want our own media. We don't want supporters, we want comrades.

And this choice is in tune with what life feels like for many today, as more and more people live in a sea of lateral social connections, enabled by personal technology that allows everyone to connect and share, in real-time, what matters most to them.

This style of protest, which some people call "horizontalism" because of its rejection of top-down leadership and followership, wasn't invented in New York in 2011.[58] Parts of the North American movements for civil rights, women's rights, peace, environmentalism, gay rights, and against globalization have long practiced non-hierarchical organization and direct democracy. Affinity groups and their methods of consensus decision-making go back to the Quakers. And formations ranging from Germany's "Unmovable Mass" movement, to Argentinean factory squatters, to the *indignados* of Spain and Greece have all used similar methods. Indeed, it was in part because of individuals from Argentina, Spain, and Greece who were present during the pre-planning meetings in New York that these practices were embedded in the Occupy movement.

These are not leaderless or structure-less phenomena. Contrary to Jo Freeman's famous critique of internal problems in the feminist movement, which she titled the "Tyranny of Structurelessness," these movements are seeking "structures of tyrannylessness," says sociologist Darcy Leach. "The question isn't whether or not to have a structure, but what kind of structure to have that will maximize participation and prevent anyone from dominating the group."⁵⁹ This way of working can be seductive, even life-changing. And as the Occupy movement has spread around the world, feeding on people's unhappiness with the banking collapse, its participatory nature has drawn in many people. To me, what is most intriguing is how this style of decision-making, which echoes how the Internet itself was originally engineered, might now be spread. This is not just because the Internet has made it easier for these movements to spread their ideas—the net may now become a platform itself for working this way.

Before Occupy reached all the way across the world to New Zealand in mid-October 2011, twenty-nine-year-old Benjamin Knight had been involved in some community organizing and social justice projects. Prior to that, he had been working on a Ph.D. on cumulative cultural evolution, doing fieldwork in Texas teaching chimps to use touch-screens. "It was an interesting research topic," he later told me, "but it felt irresponsible to stay in a system where the pace of translating that knowledge into real action was painful, when I could look around and see how much was going wrong in the world."

When Occupy happened, "I got really sucked in," he recalled. "A bunch of us in Wellington were involved in the solidarity movement with Occupy Wall Street and occupied the town square here. It was the first time I was exposed to collective decision-making on a large scale." They taught themselves how by watching online videos showing how people in Zuccotti Park in New York City were making decisions.

To Knight, the "general assembly" process was initially exhilarating: "In a way where everyone feels heard, empowered, equal to everyone else, in a public setting where people don't know each other, I've never seen anything like that."

But he also learned quickly that direct democracy and consensus decision-making was hard to sustain. "The dark side of that is that meetings last five hours, the process breaks down, and everyone can walk away feeling disempowered and pissed off.

"We had 300 people in the square, but they should have numbered in the tens of thousands," Knight reflected. Something was wrong in how the procedure was structured. The answer, he felt, might lie in harnessing online tools to make it easier for people to join in without making them camp in the square. "The way to get them to participate is to break down the practical barriers of time and geography," he said. "Needing everyone to be in the same place at the same time limits the accessibility of the process."

When the Occupy movement collapsed in New Zealand, Knight and several of his friends were still energized. And they thought there must be a way to take the best part of the general assembly process and design software that could enable groups of people, even dispersed by time and space, to work the same way. That idea became a platform called Loomio, which may be one of the most significant new tools to emerge from Occupy's ashes.

The name, Knight said, is "a nonsense word that wasn't already taken." But it's meant to signify a collaborative process. "A loom refers to weaving multiple threads together into a coherent whole," he explained. "It also refers to the illumination that comes from collective wisdom."

Knight and his fellow organizers reached out to a local network of social enterprises called Enspiral, and asked them if they could build a tool that would enable general assemblies to run better. Instead, he recalled, "They said we should build it for them, so their businesses could run better."

Starting in January 2012, the Loomio team, which had turned itself into a worker's cooperative, got a desk at Enspiral's office and started working, with three core developers doing the coding and Knight and others working on the effort's social enterprise model, its legal structure, and soon, also managing inquiries from the many local and international clients interested in using it.

At its core, Loomio is very simple. First, it makes it easy for anyone in a Loomio group to initiate a topic for conversation. And second, it makes it easy for any group member to offer a proposal up for a vote. You can vote yes, no, abstain, or block, as in a face-to-face consensus meeting process (a block is stronger than a no vote, and can stop a group in its tracks; it is meant to be used only when a participant has serious objections to a proposal and wants to make sure they are heard before a decision is made). The software puts the vote results into a pie-chart, so at any point in the conversation about a decision, members of the group can see what the group as a whole is thinking. That's it. It's also easy for a group member to form a sub-group, like a committee that works on a narrower topic area.

Discussion starts

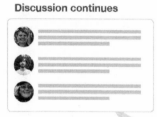

Viv proposes ...

Discussion continues

Ben proposes ...

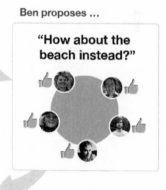

Outcome

"Let's get packing!"

"The key," said Knight, "is building shared understanding before a decision is reached by the group." He added, "That means that when you get to the outcome, it's not that everyone has to agree to the outcome, they just have to agree that its the best outcome the group can reach at that time."

As of early 2013, Loomio had more than 2,500 beta testers using it in nearly 400 groups. By the end of the year, that had more than tripled, to 8,000 people in 1,200 groups spread across thirty countries. Many users are in New Zealand and include local government entities, community groups, environmental organizations, and senior centers. For example, the Wellington City Council used it for a month-long public consultation to develop a city-wide alcohol management strategy. Bar owners, students, residents, liquor industry workers, emergency services staff, teens, and anti-alcohol campaigners were all invited to join groups of 50, along with council staff.

Generation Zero, a youth movement in New Zealand trying to fight climate change, invited 80 of its most active members to use Loomio for strategic decision-making. The Playcentre Federation is using the tool to help coordinate its network of early childhood centers around the country.

Loomio is also being embraced by a growing number of innovative political organizations around the world. For example, take the worldwide community of coders that is working on Diaspora, the user-centric alternative to Facebook that burst onto the tech scene in 2010 with a popular Kickstarter campaign. Though it has struggled since then, hobbled by the suicide of one its co-founders, now Sean Tilley, another of the original Diaspora coders, has been using Loomio to host a community of 250 people who want to help revive the project.

He told me that they are using the platform because "We needed a better way to communicate as a community and have a better way to illustrate how we felt about certain issues, policies, and solutions as a whole. We had mailing lists and GitHub issues in the past, but the barrier of entry was a little high for our non-technical users that still wanted to contribute ideas."

Tilley said the Diaspora folks had considered using other decision-making tools, but they didn't like them. He said, "Apps like Bettermeans Tracker are more about assigning tasks in an issue tracker, whereas Loomio focuses more on decisions as a community. Loomio has this great idea of establishing a culture of rule by consensus." He added, "It's helped our community be very open and democratic, and we can get a lot of great perspectives from community members on how they feel about a policy or decision. It's great, because that approach helps us make more informed decisions than majority-rule voting."

As word spread, a long waiting list of organizations hoping to get access to the tool has formed. "Everything from a contemporary rock band in Germany to an Open Business network in Bulgaria to Pirate Party movements in India and China to the Five-Star movement in Italy to eco-villages in the UK to a retail services supplier to WalMart, to P2P lab networks in Greece, local government authorities all over New Zealand, a political party in Hungary, and everything in between," Knight reported. Buoyed by local users, the tool is being translated into fourteen languages, including Hungarian, Romanian, Bulgarian and Ukrainian. The Greek Direct Democracy Alliance has set up 461 separate Loomio groups, one for every government district, to open up a conversation about how to fix their ailing country.

Loomio doesn't eliminate the need for smart community moderation; groups using the tool still need to have shared norms about their purpose and practices. But unlike many social software projects that start out by offering random people a place to congregate and then invariably fail, Loomio has taken a smarter development path by first offering to host discussions for well-defined groups of people who all have something in common with each other.

"I don't think public decision making is the best place to start," said Knight. "Since even decision-making among small groups with shared purposes is hard too, that's the place to start. If we can nail that, and create a system that is really accessible that allows more people to share in decisions together, that would be great." But Knight has a much more breath-taking vision for Loomio's long-range impact. "If you can then enable autonomous groups with great decision-making processes to then come together to make decisions together, then the need for the centralized decision making systems may melt away."[60]

"Online deliberation is remarkably hard, and somewhere between difficult and impossible using lowest-common-denominator online tools like email, surveys, etc," commented

Jon Stahl, when I asked him about Loomio's prospects. Stahl, who lives in Seattle, is a veteran online strategist who is the director of strategy at ActionSprout, a social sharing tool. "It's particularly bad in any sort of public governance process, where participation is open-to-the-public, and the participants have little prior history together and expect minimal future collaboration."[61]

Steven Clift, the founder of E-Democracy.org, agreed that there is a pressing need for better tools for group self-organization. "I have a strong interest in the now 'do something' tool kit," he commented. "I do see 'adhocracy' emerge on our local online neighborhood forums where someone says something like 'I'd like to see a community garden' and after a flurry of 'me too' notes, that person goes 'gulp, I guess I better act on my idea . . . and call an in-person meeting.'" Clift's point is that action often falters because people often drop off at that point, since face-to-face meetings require a much higher personal commitment of time and attention.

He added, "The question I have is what online tools can we either point people to or integrate into our platform that are simple enough to support sustained 'group coordination' and not suffer from the 'I won't sign up for anything new' barrier." Today's answer is pretty messy. "Right now I say to people, create a private online group/mailing list, use Google Docs, and then use the Neighbors Forum to report back on activities, gather public input when needed, and to promote your in-person meetings. Part of me thinks, despite being local, that an initial telephone teleconference building up to an in-person meeting (or, if there is distance, a Google Hangout meeting) followed by a tool set/ advice for distributing tasks, tracking progress, and reporting back to the group would be very useful. The key thing to avoid is leader/all on one shoulders burn-out while still embracing the value of e-infused leadership."[62]

Left on their own, most groups don't have a clue how to govern themselves effectively. Billy Wimsatt, the founder of the League of Young Voters and co-founder of Rebuild the Dream, agrees: "I've been a part of a handful of efforts to facilitate local self-organizing, and my sad conclusion is that when you encourage people to get together and form groups, you're essentially setting them up to get bogged down in process and power struggles that make people never want to be part of a movement again." He added, "If there was some way to scale good group process, it could be very helpful in facilitating self-organizing."[63]

This is why an elegant platform like Loomio could be so revolutionary. After a year of beta-testing, the Loomio team is tweaking its design to make it easier for people to participate in a decision, even without having to be part of a Loomio group beforehand. Watching their users, they've realized that the basic unit of participation is actually joining in a decision, not a group. "The core purpose is to make it as easy as possible for as many people as possible to participate in the decisions that affect them," Knight concluded.[64]

Loomio isn't the only venture into the community decision-making arena to watch. Charlie DeTar, a web developer and recent graduate of the MIT Media Lab, maintains a collection of simple tools to help cooperatives and affinity groups at InterTwinkles.org. A public deliberation tool built by Travis Kriplean and colleagues at the University of Washington called Consider.it was used to power a 2013 voter guide built by citizen participation, and is now being turned into a start-up. ReasonWell.com is a new platform designed to be a clearinghouse for public debate on any topic. GitHub, a collaboration platform for software developers, is beginning to be used for open deliberation of other kinds of common documents, even government policy.

And then there is Liquid Feedback, a tool that was first adopted by the German Pirate Party as a flexible way for members to participate in party policy questions, which is now being used by branches of the party in other countries as well as the anti-political Five Star Movement in Italy. Like Loomio, it is free for others to use, but requires a much greater level of understanding on the part of its users. Any member can suggest a policy, and if it gets quorum level of support within a set time period, then it goes into a debate framework. At that point, other members can make alternative proposals, and at the end members vote for their favorite. The genius of the system is that any participant can delegate their vote to someone else, so if you trust a particular person who is more expert on a topic, you can give them your proxy and they have more votes. But at any time, a member can revoke that proxy as well. The Pirate Party calls the result "Liquid Democracy" because it's in theory more fluid than representative systems but doesn't require that every person take part in every decision, as in a direct democracy.[65]

Big Data for Democracy

While platforms like SeeClickFix show how to knit together civic life in a new participatory and transparent way, and tools like Loomio promise to give people a much more effective way to deliberate and make decisions together, these bottom-up transformations in how we govern ourselves are still occurring in a world where some people know much more about us than we do about them. But there are ways to make Big Data work for all of us.

In 2011, the Ocean Conservancy, a forty-year-old advocacy group, decided that it wanted to create a "war room" for the U.S. marine conservation community that would monitor public attention with respect to ocean issues and lead timely campaigns to raise awareness. Armed with a million-dollar seed grant from the Waitt Foundation, they hired thirty-six-year-old Rachel Weidinger, then the head of international marketing for TechSoup and a longtime "communications for good" professional. But instead of asking her to promote the Ocean Conservancy and its initiatives, Weidinger was given a much broader assignment: "to condition the climate for change" in ocean-related activism and to do so in a way that was "brand agnostic."

Instead of worrying whether a particular group or spokesperson was getting attention, Upwell's staff was given the opportunity to look at the big picture of what drives public attention to the ocean and how to empower anyone who is evangelizing against climate crisis, acidification, over-fishing, and the like. This has allowed Upwell to develop an entirely different approach to using data and email that completely alters the inherently top-down dynamics of Big Data and Big Email campaigning.

What Weidinger and her staff of seven are doing is a new kind of online political organizing, one that strives to understand all the ways individuals and groups now participate in political life, grabs hold of the moments and moods that move people, and pro-actively and cooperatively weaves an open network of coordinated effort out of the usual cacophony. It's an experiment, but the early data they're sharing is quite suggestive.

Upwell starts with what Weidinger calls "big listening." Using a variety of tools, they're tracking all "social mentions" of the ocean anywhere in English. That includes tweets, public Facebook posts, blog posts, comments, mentions on message boards and forums, mainstream news coverage, and to some degree even photo and video tagging. A big chunk of their budget—$60,000 a year—goes to Radian6, a social media monitoring service that is mainly used by well-heeled corporate clients.

"Upwell tracks social mentions because they're a concrete action," Weidinger says on the group's website. "Creating a blog post, retweeting, or posting a video is a bigger deal than just viewing content. We track ocean content creators. These makers drive the online conversation."

Using Radian6's tools, Upwell's staff built keyword sets around eight key ocean subjects: marine protected areas, sustainable seafood, ocean acidification, overfishing, the Gulf of Mexico, tuna, sharks, and cetaceans. In some cases, they paid for data going back as far as three years, and from that they were able to build a set of baselines for the median level of public mentions for each of these topics. This then enabled Upwell to quickly notice when an event or some other stimulus appears to be causing the ocean-related conversation to spike.

Most communications efforts have no idea whether their work is moving the public, beyond the same gross measures that one might get with polling. How much does culture play a role in shifting public opinion? Can local stories or scandals influence people's views as much as national ones? Which public figures make waves? What words or phrases get the most attention from the public? Are there specific individuals or demographic subgroups who are especially tuned into particular parts of the public conversation and especially capable, through their own social media activity, of influencing it? Are there kinds of content that advocacy groups can generate that will move more seamlessly into the social media conversation? And how can this content be designed to advance campaign objectives?

Until recently, it would have been impossible to answer any of these questions without an astronomical budget. And indeed, before the rise of ubiquitous connectivity, social media, and the real-time news stream, there wouldn't even have been much hard data to analyze. Nor would there have been much to do with that analysis, because a few elite gatekeepers guarded the channels for moving messages. But today's media environment has been radically changed, and it's time for civic-minded organizations to update their media strategies accordingly. More than that: it's possible to give the public a three-dimensional view of the ebbs and flows of its own varied thinking, information that used to be monopolized in the hands of campaign managers alone.

Or, as Weidinger puts it, "We can do 'movement-level' metrics, not just organizational metrics." And by helping an entire movement understand what really drives conversation and interest, she and her team are learning how to reach broader audiences.

Upwell's biggest discovery from its ocean social mention analysis was this: the public loves sharks. Note: loves, not fears. While the Upwell team is wary of so-called "sentiment analysis," their analysis of prominent word pairings discovered that the bulk of social mentions of sharks were celebratory ("sharks are awesome!") with less than a quarter emphasizing people's fears. They also found that "Shark Week," the Discovery Channel's annual August marketing blitz, was far and away the most consequential time of the year for mentions of sharks: "the Superbowl of shark," in Weidinger's words. In 2011, there were more than 740,000 social mentions of sharks that week, compared to between 40,000 and 70,000 a week during the rest of the year.

Armed with this historical data and insight, Upwell decided to hold a series of "sharkinars" for marine conservation communications staffers, to help them prepare for the next year's Shark Week, which they predicted could be three times as big as in

2011. Or, as their blog put it, "when you see that fin-shaped spike, it's time to get into the (social media) water."[66]

"Traditionally," Weidinger told me, "the conservation sector has viewed Shark Week as horribly sensationalized. But we were, like, this is the high point of people talking about sharks all year."

So Upwell posted detailed tips on how best to wade into the conversation without turning people off (share the celebration, for starters). They also mined their data and blogged in advance about the top influencers in the marine conservation arena, to help knit free agents into the network. And finally, they collected and curated a smorgasbord of photos and infographics that groups could use most successfully for social sharing during Shark Week. After all that preparation, "We asked people what their plans were and let them just share what they were planning, rather than pushing them to all retweet the same thing," Weidinger added. All of this was done out in the open, by the way.

In other words, Upwell used Shark Week to foster a network of formal and informal influencers and engaged them in advance with useful tips and content. And they got results. While the overall Shark Week conversation grew by 109 percent according to Radian6's data, to nearly two million mentions, the shark conservation community's share of that grew by an even greater amount, 210 percent. The people Upwell engaged not only participated more, they were mentioned more by other participants in the much larger overall conversation.[67]

Was this just a drop in the ocean? According to Weidinger, "The idea is that Upwell's work with online attention will significantly increase public awareness of the crisis the ocean is facing. With this new base, we hope to give ocean policy work and consumer behavior campaigns some serious footing to stand on. Finally."

An earlier initiative around World Oceans Day, the previous June, taught the Upwell team some subtle lessons about how best to get organizations that ostensibly have the same goals, but also must compete for attention, to work in tandem. "We made a huge mistake in that campaign in trying to get everyone to use the same hashtag, #worldoceansday," Weidinger told me.

"We were talking to all the mid-level communications people at these organizations," she noted "For most of them, social media is an email list-building device. They all had siloed campaigns they were running on World Oceans Day."

Weidinger recounted trying to get them to all work together. "'Sorry'," we were told, 'we can't even retweet you.'" Each group wanted their own hashtag to be the one used, reinforcing their organization's brand rather than the broader common one. On the basis of that experience, she decided "it would be crazy to spend years getting to the point where people can retweet each other."[68] That insight led straight into the revamped approach Upwell took around Shark Week, sharing everyone's efforts and making sure participants knew why coalescing around particular themes and terms would be important. By being totally open about their findings, they effectively pulled the ocean conservation groups into participation.

The "Tide Report," Upwell's daily email, is another evolving tool in its portfolio. Geared for busy communications professionals who work on ocean issues, along with "social media nerds" and evangelists, it's a small, hand-made list of big communicators.

This curated email is really one of Weidinger's obsessions. As it got going, she had a staff intern mail a thank-you postcard to every individual who signed up—many of whom still remember the touch. People who opened the emails religiously got a weekly postcard. She and her staff zealously track their daily open rates, going so far as to use an app that plays an audio ping in their office every time one of their key influencers clicks "open." These kinds of personal social metrics are king at Upwell.

And so is experimentation. If you read Upwell's blog, and in particular the posts coming out of its "Attention Lab," you'll find yourself invited into a fairly open process of trial and error. When an article called "The Ocean Is Broken" came out in Australia's Newcastle *Herald* and proceeded to blow up online (shared more than 115,000 times on Facebook and Twitter in less than a month, with close to an equal number of comments), the Upwell team dug in to figure out why it went so big.[69] The answers included everything from the personal nature of the story, which retraced one yachtsman's 3,000-mile trek across the Pacific and his discovery that much of the wildlife he remembered from past journeys had disappeared, to the story's unexpectedly moving title. "'Broken' isn't a word we're used to hearing in the context of the ocean—it's poetic, symbolic, and new to our lexicon," Upwell's Ray Dearborn blogged.[70] A look at a comparison between mainstream media coverage of the Kardashians and ocean acidification produced the bemused discovery that simply including the celebrities in the study probably produced a big spike in online discussion of the more serious issue.[71] In sharing these findings, Upwell isn't just showing off its smarts—it's drawing other smart social media practitioners into its internal conversation, which can only make everyone a bit smarter.

The techniques and savvy that Weidinger and her team are learning, modeling, and deploying have uses far beyond the ocean issue. It would be pretty interesting if more funders copied Ted Waitt and the Waitt Foundation and seeded similarly open, brand-agnostic listening and campaigning hubs for other issues. Imagine an OpenWell for the transparency movement, or an UpStrike for labor. Instead of the system we now have, where Big Data is closely guarded by a handful of closed organizations and Big Email is used by small teams of advocates to speak for large numbers of people, entire sectors of the advocacy arena could be transformed.

How we use Big Data across society is a huge question beyond the scope of this book. As author and consultant Alistair Croll wrote in 2012, it is "our generation's civil rights issue, and we don't know it."[72] He pointed out that while it is against the law to discriminate against people in housing or banking decisions based on race, credit card companies have other ways to achieve similar ends. For example, he cited a report from someone who had their credit limit at a store lowered, based on the fact that other people who shop at the same places as that person had poor repayment histories. OkCupid, the online dating service, posted a list of words that its white users say they like, which Croll noted could be easily used to figure out, with a high degree of certainty, what someone's race was based on the things they mention on Facebook or Twitter.

At the same time, if we insist on transparency about what is being collected and how it is being used, and we demand as much access as possible to publicly-generated data (minus personal identifiers), Big Data can also be used to inform us about ourselves in incredibly valuable ways. For example, by getting the addresses of people in prison, the Justice Mapping project discovered that certain blocks in particular neighborhoods in cities like New York and New Orleans were, in effect, "million-dollar blocks." That is, government was spending that much per year, to imprison a handful of people from those specific locations. In the case of New Orleans, this discovery helped persuade the city government to pay for local job training and other intervention programs focused in particular neighborhoods.[73] Eventually, the state also decided to liberalize some of its sentencing and corrections policies, reducing the number of people thrown back in jail for minor parole violations.[74]

If we want, we can bend technology to serve the end of a more participatory democracy, to start building the institutions of the future. We can achieve a much greater level of collective self-awareness and self-governance. We can transform the partial, opaque, and manipulated forms of democracy and participation that we experience today. But to get there we also have to change our own behavior and the expectations we place on the technologies that shape our daily lives.

Coda: The Trouble We Face; The Opportunity We Have

I love the Internet; it helps us find the others.
I hate the Internet; it helps others find out about us.

When I first sat down to write this book, the name "Edward Snowden" meant nothing. As I began, the first stories about the National Security Agency's massive surveillance programs were reported by Glenn Greenwald in *The Guardian* and then Barton Gellman and Laura Poitras in *The Washington Post*.

Greenwald's scoop revealed the agency's collection of telephone records of millions of American customers of Verizon, and included the text of a current secret court order authorizing the practice.[1] Then Gellman and Poitras in the *Post*, along with Greenwald and his colleague Ewen MacAskill in the *Guardian*, broke the even bigger story of the Prism program, through which the NSA and Britain's GCHQ were collecting the search histories, emails, file transfers, and live chats of users of Google, Facebook, Apple, Microsoft, Yahoo, and other major U.S. tech platforms.[2]

Greenwald, Poitras, and MacAskill flew to Hong Kong and produced an even more amazing story. The source of these leaks, Edward Snowden, a former NSA contractor, gave them an on-the-record interview explaining his motivations. "I don't want to live in a world where there's no privacy and therefore no room for intellectual exploration and creativity," he said. What the NSA is doing, he said, posed "an existential threat to democracy," adding that, "The government has granted itself powers it is not entitled to. There is no public oversight."[3]

As the story has unspooled, we have learned that:

- The NSA is collecting the "metadata"—meaning the time, date, duration and numbers called—of nearly every phone call made in America and storing that information for five years.
- The NSA also collects the metadata of Americans' Internet usage, including who they send and receive emails from, their IP addresses, what web pages they visit, even their use of Google Maps, and stores that information for at least a year.
- People up to three "hops" from someone who is reasonably connected to a foreign terror group can come under greater scrutiny, without a specific court order. That is, if you are someone who called or emailed someone who called or emailed someone who was in contact with a suspect, your metadata is fair game for the NSA to analyze.

- The NSA uses all this data to create social network graphs mapping Americans' social connections, locations, traveling companions, and other information.
- The secret court overseeing these programs has found many violations of its rules and also admitted that it has difficulty managing the scale of the oversight required.
- The NSA and GCHQ (Britain's spy agency) have covertly worked to insert weaknesses in online encryption standards used to protect the privacy of personal and commercial data.
- Both agencies act in completely unfettered ways to collect massive amounts of data on people all over the world, and not only in countries that are adversaries of the U.S. or the U.K., but allies as well.
- In at least one and possibly as many as six countries, the NSA records and retains the content of all the phone calls made there going back at least a month in time, allowing the agency to "rewind and review conversations" for retrospective surveillance.[4]

While all of this was unfolding, in July 2013, Chelsea Manning (the former Bradley Manning), who admitted leaking massive government databases on the Iraq war, the Afghanistan war, and many State Department internal cables, was sentenced to thirty-five years in prison for violating the Espionage Act, the Computer Fraud and Abuse Act, stealing government property, and disobeying orders.

It is impossible to write a book about the Internet and politics in America, the role of data and the future of democracy, without addressing the NSA files, state surveillance and the broader ways the United States government has been dealing with whistleblowers and other trouble-makers. Since my previous book, *WikiLeaks and the Age of Transparency*, looked optimistically at the rise of sousveillance, our ability to collectively watch from below the powers that be, it seems right to end this book with some discussion of what we might learn from Edward Snowden's courageous revelations as well as the treatment of Manning and other whistleblowers.

When I wrote *WikiLeaks and the Age of Transparency* at the beginning of 2012, I was trying to situate the actions of both Julian Assange and Manning in the context of a much larger movement for greater political transparency. I still think that connection technologies are disruptive to traditional power structures and, in the long run, we will get to a new equilibrium where ordinary people gain more power over their institutions. Someday, we will be able to effectively watch and influence our government, politicians, and corporations as much as they can watch and influence us. However, it's impossible to deny that what we've seen and learned over the last two years is fundamentally challenging to this goal and hope.

It is good Manning was acquitted of the ridiculous and dangerous charge of "aiding the enemy." But her treatment and trial should still leave us very concerned about the state of freedom in America today. When Daniel Ellsberg turned himself in after leaking the Pentagon Papers (which were all "Top Secret"—a level of classification that Manning did not breach), he was charged with various crimes and then allowed to go free on bail, free to speak to the country, until his trial. Manning was put in very harsh solitary conditions, well beyond what was warranted by her status as a soldier. Coverage of her trial was constrained by a court that wouldn't make transcripts available, and her defense was prevented from offering evidence showing that she did not harm the country. One would think there should have been more of an outcry on her behalf (and there has been some), but there was no one in our bipartisan political establishment willing to challenge the notion that she was a hacker and a traitor. Even Democrats who were vociferously anti-Iraq War, and who have questioned the war in Afghanistan and our diplomatic coziness with dictators around the world, had nothing to say in defense of Manning's leaks.

Manning's treatment is part of a larger war on leaks by the Obama administration, which veteran journalist Leonard Downie recently called "the most aggressive I've seen since the Nixon administration, when I was one of the editors involved in *The Washington Post*'s investigation of Watergate." Downie authored a major report on the Obama administration and the press for the Committee to Protect Journalists, and his findings are deeply worrisome.[5] Not only has Obama pursued more whistleblowers than all his predecessors combined, but in the wake of the WikiLeaks revelations, his administration formed an "Insider Threat Task Force" to more rigorously police the behavior of government employees with access to classified information. *McLatchy Newspapers*'s reporters Marisa Taylor and Jonathan S. Landay found that some agencies were now pursing "unauthorized disclosures of any information, not just classified material . . . millions of federal employees and contractors must watch for 'high-risk persons or behaviors' among co-workers and could face penalties, including criminal charges, for failing to report them. Leaks to media are equated with espionage."[6]

And that gets me to Snowden. Here I am more hopeful about the potential for reform. The NSA's overreach is generating a strong response from civil libertarians on both sides of the aisle—as has been illustrated by the close House vote in the summer of 2013 on an amendment to stop mass surveillance and require a court order to collect an individual's metadata.[7] Roughly half of Americans say they think Snowden should be considered a hero, which is substantial considering that no one beyond a few gutsy members of Congress have voiced that opinion.[8] A federal district court judge, Richard Leon, has ruled that the bulk collection of phone metadata is likely unconstitutional, explaining in easy-to-understand language that past legal precedent allowing the usage of such information without a warrant was out of date. As he wrote, "The ubiquity of phones has dramatically altered the quantity of information that is now available and, more importantly, what that information can tell the government about people's lives. . . . Put simply, people in 2013 have an entirely different relationship with phones than they did thirty-four years ago."[9]

The extent of the government's surveillance programs is alarming. Authoritarianism can rise in any country, even America. Even if "the good guys" are overseeing the NSA, there is no justification for limitless data collection in a democracy. It's too much concentrated power to be in the hands of any government, and such a mass of information invites abuse against the powerless. The knowledge that all our digital communications and behaviors are being monitored and stored for potential later analysis is already a form of behavior control. I shouldn't have to think or act differently if I have had contact with people like Julian Assange or Glenn Greenwald as part of my work. Furthermore, any activist or organization seeking fundamental social or economic change must now also act according to this knowledge: if you are deemed a threat to the established order, these tools may be used to constrain your actions too.

Unfortunately, as of this writing, few organizations beyond the ACLU, the Electronic Frontier Foundation, Free Press and Credo Mobile have prioritized challenging the dragnet surveillance policies of the national security state. Groups like MoveOn which pride themselves on their progressivism, have done very little—a reflection of the fact that their members, who are mostly liberal Democrats, don't think this is an important concern. This is terribly short-sighted. In 2017, the person at the helm in the White House may have a very different attitude toward civil liberties and dissent. And mass surveillance chills speech. If the police announced that they were taking pictures and keeping records of every person who attended a legal political rally, just in case someday they needed to know who was politically active, we would be rightfully outraged. Mass collection and storage of our digital activities is no different.

This February, I visited Berlin to speak at a conference that was called, somewhat ponderously, "As Darkness Falls: Theory and Practice of Self-Empowerment in the Age of Digital Control." In advance of my trip and in preparation for this gloomy topic, I decided to put myself in the shoes of someone who wanted as much privacy as possible, while still being able to use a phone and the Internet. At a minimum, I thought it was time to learn, as a journalist, what it takes to be able to have secure communications with a source. What I found both heartened me and also angered me.

The good news is that if you want to protect your privacy and still use digital tools, encryption can protect you. As Snowden himself pointed out during his talk in March at the South by Southwest Festival in Austin, when he beamed in via somewhere in Russia, even the NSA, which has a whole task force targeting him, has not been able to find out what he gave to the journalists he leaked to.[10]

Not only does encryption work, but it is becoming much easier for a non-technically minded person to implement. Mobile apps like TextSecure, ChatSecure, K-9 Mail, and LinPhone can give you the same functionalities of texting, chatting, emailing and calling that you have with a regular phone, and an app called Orbot will enable you to surf the web from the phone through Tor, the anonymizing browser.

But using encryption to protect yourself has a number of serious drawbacks. First, until it becomes more of a mainstream activity, people who choose to lock their digital secrets are, in effect, painting a target on their doors for would-be snoops. (This is one reason why people who think they personally have "nothing to hide" should still use browsers like Tor—to make it easier for the people who have a justified need for privacy to stand out less.) Second, while it's great to be able to do a one-way activity like surfing the web without leaving a digital trail, most of the other things we do online involve other people. Personally encrypting your own emails offers little protection if none of your friends or contacts also are willing to learn how to use encryption.

Unfortunately, choosing to maximize your protection from unwanted snooping means also cutting yourself off from the very thing that makes the Networked Age so alluring. Unlike four years ago, when I was stranded in Berlin by an ashcloud from Iceland and buoyed by my ambient online connections to friends and strangers alike, on this trip to Berlin I felt cut off from a vibrant and important part of my life. I had shut off Twitter, avoided Facebook, and emailed only the few people who I had exchanged PGP keys with. I was relatively anonymous, but I was also disconnected and out of touch. It was as if a piece of my personality had been shut off.

This is no way to live. Expecting everyone to wear the digital equivalent of body armor is no solution to the problem of mass surveillance.We need a rebalancing of America's priorities and a clearer sense of what truly threatens us. We have allowed a largely secret national security apparatus to grow enormously since 9-11, while the number of terrorist plots that the NSA claims to have prevented numbers, at best, in the dozens. Meanwhile, hundreds of thousands of Americans die prematurely every year from preventable hospital errors or a basic lack of health insurance. Our fear of terrorism is out of proportion to the real threat.

It's not enough to decry the overreaching practices of government. We also need to worry about our own tendency to value convenience over privacy. The privacy desert we're living in now, where so much information is so easily obtained, has been built largely on extremely weak privacy practices that we all casually submit to as we surf the web, post to Facebook, and use our mobile phones. It is good that major tech companies are all now taking steps to build stronger encryption into their web services, since they can theoretically do much more to reverse the current trend than individuals acting on their own. But there's an inherent problem in expecting the same companies that give us free online tools while they mine our data and sell advertising alongside our email and Facebook posts to go as far as they can to restore individual privacy. An encrypted email, after all, is not one Google can read either, for the purposes of targeted advertising.

Likewise, we must press our elected representatives to answer for how they use our personal data in their political campaigns. The big voter files that have become so valuable to the major parties exist in a kind of privacy netherworld. The use of Big Data in campaigns is protected by the First Amendment, of course. But in the same way that Congress has enacted transparency rules governing the use of money in politics, it's time to consider some similar regulations for the use of voter data. As more politicians get elected by using Big Data to manage and manipulate voters with total precision, will any of them show any appetite to regulate its use? Only if voters and the press start asking questions about it.

Obviously, we can no longer take for granted the liberatory, democratizing potential of the Internet. I find myself agreeing with security expert Bruce Schneier, who says we are in a "battle for power on the Internet." In the early days of the network's spread, upstarts, mavericks, and independents were the first to grasp its potential and swifter to adapt, amplifying their own power and disrupting many established institutions. But now even more powerful actors, like governments and big corporations, are also adjusting. "The truth is that technology magnifies power in general," Schneier writes, but "when the already-powerful big institutions finally figured out how to harness the Internet, they had more power to magnify."[11]

These are strange times. It is a contradictory moment in American political life, defined by rapid technological transformation, national public-policy gridlock, and revelations of yet another layer of secret government that still largely operates unhindered by our normal system of checks and balances. Ordinary citizens feel more powerless than ever as they watch their elected leaders struggle and fail to get anything done in the face of organized political minorities. We're distracted and confused. Each day seems to bring a new tech innovation that puts more computing power in our hands but also threatens to enslave us.

Nonetheless, I remain optimistic about our chances. Decentralized power, in the long run, will prove stronger than centralized power—but only if we keep pressing for more effective ways to coordinate our distributed energies and passions. Find the others.

FIGURE I.

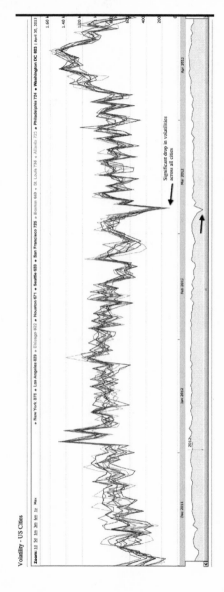

FIGURE 2.

BLOG for America
The Official Howard Dean Weblog

Thursday, October 09, 2003

Open Thread #2

After all, it's only 10 pm on the West Coast. This is your space.

Posted by **Mathew Gross** at 01:09 AM
Link | Mail This Entry to a Friend | TrackBack (0) | Comments (113)

Wednesday, October 08, 2003

Open Thread

Use this thread to talk about the day's news.

Don't forget to make plans to watch the DNC debate on CNN tomorrow night at 8 pm Eastern. And, if you live in Phoenix, you can join Governor Dean at a rally and debate-watching party by clicking here.

Posted by **Mathew Gross** at 09:07 PM
Link | Mail This Entry to a Friend | TrackBack (0) | Comments (356)

Iowa Report: Urgent!

November 15th is *the* day in the battle for the Iowa Caucuses. All the candidates, and a huge gathering of caucus goers, the people who decide who gets out of Iowa with their presidential hopes alive, will be in one place on one night. Out of a 7300 seats, only 1000 balcony seats and 800 table seats are left. Can you feel me on this? Buy a ticket and join us if you can. Buy a ticket for the campaign to give away if you can't make it. (Balcony West and North are best) Both can be done online **www.iowademocrats.org**, but only if you buy it RIGHT NOW!!

Posted by **Clare Gannon** at 06:38 PM
Link | Mail This Entry to a Friend | TrackBack (0) | Comments (154)

Dean for America Launches Petition for Domestic Violence Awareness Month

WASHINGTON, D.C.--In honor of Domestic Violence Awareness Month, Dean for America launched a **petition**

Rally for Dean!
Thursday, 10/9 in Phoenix

Sign the Petition:
End violence against women

461,206
AMERICANS 4 DEAN
▸ *Join today!* ◂

meetup 180,000!

Invite your friends to join the campaign!

Contribute ▸
HELP TAKE BACK OUR COUNTRY

Posters for America
Download, Print, Post, Share: Spread the word about Howard Dean.

GET LOCAL
Find other Dean events in your area

FEEDBACK
tell us...

ACKNOWLEDGEMENTS

I'm indebted to many people for sharing their ideas and offering their encouragement: Daniel Ben-Horin, Ben Berkowitz, Elana Berkowitz, danah boyd, Andrew Boyd, Catherine Bracy, Jake Brewer, Matthew Burton, Daniel Cantor, Tantek Celik, Steven Clift, Gabriella Coleman, Cheryl Contee, Marc Cooper, David Corn, Susan Crawford, Joe Dinkin, Stacy Donohue, David Donnelly, Sam Dorman, Shannon Dosemagen, Esther Dyson, Zack Exley, Allison Fine, Natalie Foster, Nathan Freitas, Marshall Ganz, Jim Gilliam, Dan Gillmor, Tom Glaisyer, Seth Godin, Joe Goldman, Lawrence Goodwyn, Nick Grossman, Scott Heiferman, Peter Hirshberg, Ilyse Hogue, Andrew Hoppin, David Isenberg, Jeff Jarvis, Steven Johnson, Clay Johnson, Nick Judd, Mike Klein, Benjamin Knight, Daniel Kreiss, Kate Krontiris, Lawrence Lessig, Joshua Levy, Marianne Manilov, Rebecca MacKinnon, Jerry Michalski, Nicco Mele, Alia McKee, Ellen and Richard Miller, Daniel Mintz, Jason Mogus, Adam Mordecai, Craig Newmark, Beth Noveck, Eli Pariser, Richard Parker, Mark Pesce, Marko Rakar, Ethan Roeder, Jay Rosen, Douglas Rushkoff, Nancy Scola, Ryan Senser, Jessica Shearer, Clay Shirky, David Sifry, Ruby Sinreich, Bryan Sivak, Anne-Marie Slaughter, Marc Smith, Matt Stoller, Tom Steinberg, Taren Stinebrickner-Kauffman,

Zephyr Teachout, Jenny Toomey, Zeynep Tufekci, Katrina van-den Heuvel, Tim Walker, Jeff Warren, Rachel Weidinger, Michael Wesch, Billy Wimsatt, John Wonderlich, Christopher Wong, Jillian York, Deanna Zandt, and Ethan Zuckerman.

In particular, I'm very grateful to Yochai Benkler, David Karpf, Nancy Scola, and Matt Stempeck, who took time from their busy schedules to read this book in draft form and offer comments and criticism. Andrew Rasiej, my friend and partner in running Personal Democracy Media, has been a constant source of support.

To my editor and publisher, John Oakes, thank you for summoning another book out of me. Thank you, too, to copyeditor Justin Humphries and designer Courtney Andujar at OR Books.

Finally, my eternal thanks to my wife Leslie, for all of her love, and to my children Mira and Jesse, for inspiring me and also for putting up with my bad jokes.

In many ways the ideas in this book represent the culmination of years of conversation with all of these people and others whom I have not named, but I take full responsibility for all of its flaws.

NOTES

Forward

1 For further discussion of these core values, see Doc Searls and David Weinberger, "World of Ends: What the Internet Is and How to Stop Mistaking It for Something Else," http://www.worldofends.com, March 10, 2003; The Open Source Definition, http://opensource.org/osd; "8 Principles of Open Government Data," http://www.opengovdata.org/home/8principles, December 8, 2007; The Declaration of Internet Freedom, http://www.internetdeclaration.org, July 2012.

2 Vaclav Havel, "A Joint Session of the U.S. Congress," February 21, 1990, http://vaclavhavel.cz/showtrans.php?cat=projevy&val=322_aj_projevy .html&typ=HTML.

3 Ibid.

The Revolution That Wasn't

1 Searls and Weinberger, op. cit.

2 Timothy Leary: "Admit it. You aren't like them. You're not even close. You may occasionally dress yourself up as one of them, watch the same mindless television shows as they do, maybe even eat the same fast food sometimes. But it seems that the more you try to fit in, the more you feel like an outsider, watching the 'normal people' as they go about their automatic existences. For every time you say club passwords like 'Have a nice day' and 'Weather's awful today, eh?' you yearn inside to say forbidden things like 'Tell me something that makes you cry' or 'What do you think deja vu is for?' Face it, you even want to talk to that girl in the elevator. But what if that girl in the elevator (and the balding man who walks past your cubicle at work) are thinking the same thing? Who knows what you might learn from taking a chance on conversation with a stranger? Everyone carries a piece of the puzzle. Nobody comes into your life by mere coincidence. Trust your instincts. Do the unexpected. Find the others . . ."

3 Jim Gilliam, Transcript, "The Internet is My Religion," http://www.internet-ismyreligion.com/transcript.

4 "It Gets Better: Dan and Terry," It Gets Better Project YouTube channel, https://www.youtube.com/watch?v=7IcVyvg2Qlo, September 21, 2010.

5 "Joel Burns Tells Gay Teens 'It Gets Better,'" https://www.youtube.com/watch?v=ax96cghOnY4, October 13, 2010.

6   Michael Chui, et. al., "The Social Economy: Unlocking Value and Productivity Through Social Technologies," McKinsey Global Institute, July 2013, http://www .mckinsey.com/insights/high_tech_telecoms_internet/the_social_economy.

7   Douglas Rushkoff, *Present Shock* (Penguin Group, New York, NY, 2013), p. 145.

8   Ibid., p. 206.

9   Ibid., p. 72.

10 Communication with author, email, October 14, 2013.

11 "FAQ about trends on Twitter," https://support.twitter.com/articles/101125-faqs-about-trends-on-twitter.

12 "KONY 2012," Invisible Children YouTube channel, https://www.youtube.com/watch?v=Y4MnpzG5Sqc, March 5, 2012.

13 Josh Kron and J. David Goodman, "Online, A Distant Conflict Soars to Topic No. 1," *The New York Times*, March 8, 2012, http://www.nytimes.com/2012/03/09/world/africa/online-joseph-kony-and-a-ugandan-conflict-soar-to-topic-no-1.html.

14 Rajiv Chandrasekaran, "Kony 2013: U.S. Quietly Intensifies Effort to Help African Troops Capture Infamous Warlord," *The Washington Post*, October 28, 2013, http://www.washingtonpost.com/world/national-security/kony-2013-us-quietly-intensifies-effort-to-help-african-troops-capture-infamous-warlord/2013/10/28/74db9720-3cb3-11e3-b6a9-da62c264f40e_print.html.

15 Teju Cole, "The White-Savior Industrial Complex," *The Atlantic*, March 21, 2012, http://www.theatlantic.com/international/archive/2012/03/the-white-savior-industrial-complex/254843/.

16 Allyssa Newcomb, "Kony 2012 Filmmaker Jason Russell Opens Up About Nude Public Meltdown," Good Morning America, October 8, 2012, http://abcnews.go.com/US/kony-2012-filmmaker-jason-russell-opens-nude-public/story?id=17423266.

17 In fairness, the KONY 2012 video did increase Washington's awareness of the issue, and helped insure that Congress would fund continued efforts to find Kony and aid communities victimized by his forces, the Lord's Resistance Army. And the grassroots activists running Invisible Children and its sister organization, The Resolve, have continued their work aimed at stopping Kony and the LRA. They just haven't become a mass movement, despite the massive attention generated by the "KONY 2012" video.

18 See, for example, this tweet from Van Jones, co-founder of Rebuild the Dream: "WOW. This is the most impressive video advocacy campaign I have ever seen. Spread the word. KONY 2012: http://youtu.be/Y4MnpzG5Sqc via @youtube," https://twitter.com/VanJones68/status/177270733821591554.

19 Joe Trippi, *The Revolution Will Not Be Televised* (Harper Collins, New York, NY 2004), p. 57.

20 Author's notes.

21 Email from Eli Pariser and Justin Ruben of MoveOn PAC, December 9, 2004. http://www.democraticunderground.com/discuss/duboard.php?az=view_all&address=104x2808601.

22 Hugh Hewitt, *Blog: Understanding the Information Revolution That's Changing Your World* (Thomas Nelson, 2006), p. 198.

23 Yochai Benkler, *The Wealth of Networks* (Yale University Press, New Haven, 2006), p. 188.

24 Ibid, p. 11.

25 Ibid., p. 239.

26 Ibid., p. 241.

27 Ibid., p. 242.

28 Yochai Benkler, Hal Roberts, Rob Faris, Alicia Solow-Niederman, and Bruce Etling, "Social Mobilization and the Networked Public Sphere: Mapping the SOPA-PIPA Debate," Berkman Center for Internet and Society, July 19, 2012, http://papers.ssrn.com/sol3/papers.cfm?abstract_id=2295953.

29 Yochai Benkler, "A Free Irresponsible Press: WikiLeaks and the Battle Over the Soul of the Networked Fourth Estate," http://benkler.org/Benkler_Wikileaks_current.pdf.

30 Benkler, *The Wealth of Networks*, p. 253.

31 Ibid., p. 256.

32 Campaign Finance Institute, "The Cost of Winning an Election, 1986–2012," http://www.cfinst.org/pdf/vital/VitalStats_t1.pdf.

33 Campaign Finance Institute, "House Receipts from Individuals, PACS, and Other, All General Election Candidates, 1999–2010," http://www.cfinst.org/pdf/historical/Donors_HouseCand_2000–2010.pdf and Michael Malbin, Campaign Finance Institute, personal communication to author, September 2, 2013.

34 Ibid.

35 Ibid.

36 Michael Malbin, "Small Donors: Incentives, Economies of Scale, and Effects," *The Forum: A Journal of Applied Research in Contemporary Politics*, Volume 11, Issue No. 3 (October 2013).

37 Schlozman, Kay Lehman, Sidney Verba and Henry E. Brady, *The Unheavenly Chorus: Unequal Political Voice and the Broken Promise of American Democracy*, (Princeton, NJ: Princeton University Press) p. 505.

38 https://www.opensecrets.org/bigpicture/reelect.php

39 Richard Winger, "Major Parties Fail to Nominate Candidates in Almost 40 percent of State Legislative Races," *Ballot Access News*, October 25, 2012, http://www.ballot-access.org/2012/10/major-parties-fail-to-nominate-candidates-in-almost-40-of-state-legislative-races.

40 David Graeber, *The Democracy Project* (Spiegel and Grau, 2012), p. 95.

41 "Demographics of Internet Users," Pew Internet & American Life Project, April-May 2013 survey, http://pewinternet.org/Static-Pages/Trend-Data-(Adults)/Whos-Online.aspx; "Internet Adoption, 1995–2013," Pew Internet & American Life Project, http://pewinternet.org/Static-Pages/Trend-Data-(Adults)/Internet-Adoption.aspx; Maeve Duggan and Aaron Smith, "Social Media Update 2013," Pew Internet & American Life Project," December 30, 2013, http://www.pewinternet.org/2013/12/30/social-media-update-2013.

42 Holly Bailey, "How Joe Wilson's Heckle Became a Campaign Cash Cow," *Newsweek*, September 17, 2009.

43 Lindsay Young, "Outside Spenders' Return on Investment," Sunlight Foundation, December 17, 2012, http://reporting.sunlightfoundation.com/2012/return_on_investment.

44 Nick Bilton, "As User Interaction on Facebook Drops, Sharing Comes at a Cost," *The New York Times*, March 3, 2010, http://bits.blogs.nytimes.com/2013/03/03/disruptions-when-sharing-on-facebook-comes-at-a-cost.

45 Proceedings of the Twenty-Fourth Internet Engineering Task Force, July 13–17, 1992; http://www.ietf.org/old/2009/proceedings/prior29/IETF24.pdf.

Big Data: The Politics of Computational Management

1   Daniel Kreiss, *Taking Our Country Back: The Crafting of Networked Politics from Howard Dean to Barack Obama* (Oxford University Press, 2012), p. 5.

2   Micah L. Sifry, "Presidential Campaign 2012, By the Numbers," techPresident.com, November 26, 2012, http://techpresident.com/news/23178/presidential-campaign-2012-numbers.

3   Byron Tau, "President Obama's data a powerful tool for Democrats," Politico, July 9, 2013, http://www.politico.com/story/2013/07/2014-elections-president-obama-email-list-93871.html.

4   Curtis Gans, Committee for the Study of the American Electorate, November 8, 2012, http://bipartisanpolicy.org/sites/default/files/2012%20Voter%20Turnout%20Full%20Report.pdf.

5   Daniel Kreiss, op. cit., p. 53.

6   David Sifry, "State of the Blogosphere, October 2004," *Sifry's Alerts*, http://www.sifry.com/alerts/archives/000245.html.

7   Michael Malbin, Michael Malbin, "Small Donors: Incentives, Economies of Scale, and Effects," *The Forum: A Journal of Applied Research in Contemporary Politics*, Volume 11, Issue No. 3 (October 2013).

8   Patrick Taylor, "A New Power in the Streets," *The New York Times*, February 17, 2003, http://www.nytimes.com/2003/02/17/world/threats-and-responses-news-analysis-a-new-power-in-the-streets.html.

9   Mathew Gross, "Blogging for America," chapter in *Mousepads, Shoe Leather and Hope*, Teachout and Streeter, eds, (Boulder, CO, Paradigm Publishers, 2008), p. 107.

10 Interview with author, March 29, 2004.

11 Michael Malbin, "Small Donors, Large Donors and the Internet," Campaign Finance Institute, April 2009, http://www.cfinst.org/president/pdf/PresidentialWorkingPaper_April09.pdf.

12 Kreiss, op. cit., p. 166.

13 Nancy Scola, "Can Obama's Army Convert to a Peace-Time Force? Plouffe Responds," techPresident.com, November 25, 2009, http://techpresident.com/blog-entry/can-obamas-army-convert-peacetime-force-plouffe-responds.

14 Micah Sifry, "The Battle to Control Obama's MySpace," techPresident.com, May 21, 2007, http://techpresident.com/blog-entry/battle-control-obamas-myspace.

15 Kreiss, op. cit., p. 134.

16 Kreiss, op. cit. p. 137.

17 Jose Antonio Vargas, "Obama Raised Half a Billion Online," *The Washington Post*, November 20, 2008, http://voices.washingtonpost.com/44/2008/11/obama-raised-half-a-billion-on.html.

18 Nancy Scola, "With 'Dashboard,' Obama Aims to Bridge Online and Off," *The Atlantic*, May 24, 2012, http://www.theatlantic.com/politics/archive/2012/05/with-dashboard-obama-campaign-aims-to-bridge-online-and-off/257606.

19 Kreiss, op. cit., p. 158.

20 Kreiss, op. cit., p. 26.

21 David Plouffe, *The Audacity to Win* (New York: Viking, 2009), p. 364.

22 "Barack Obama in Indianapolis, IN," BarackObamadotcom YouTube channel, April 30, 2008, https://www.youtube.com/watch?v=WyNzC9W2C8Q.

23 Tim Dickinson, "The Machinery of Hope," *Rolling Stone*, March 20, 2008.

24 Ellen McGirt, "How Chris Hughes Helped Launch Facebook and the Barack Obama Campaign," *Fast Company*, April 1, 2009, http://www.fastcompany.com/node/1207594/print.

25 Amy Harder, "Obama's Conversation Starter," *National Journal*, April 14, 2009, http://www.nationaljournal.com/njonline/obama-s-conversation-starter-20090414.

26 Lisa Taddeo, "The Man Who Made Obama," *Esquire*, November 3, 2009, http://www.esquire.com/features/david-plouffe-0309.

27 Peter Wallsten, "Obama's Grass Roots In Search of New Turf," *Los Angeles Times*, December 5, 2008, http://articles.latimes.com/2008/dec/05/nation/na-obama-supporters5.

28 Miranda Neubauer, "What Organized Labor Could Learn From Occupied Wall Street," techPresident.com, December 13, 2011, http://techpresident.com/news/21482/what-organized-labor-could-learn-occupy-wall-street.

29 Sam Graham-Felsen, "What Gladwell Got Wrong: Beyond 'Like Button' Activism," The Huffington Post, October 1, 2010, http://www.huffingtonpost.com/sam-grahamfelsen/what-gladwell-got-wrong-b_b_746658.html.

30 Mark Gabrish Conlan, "President's Former Advisor Attacks Him at Freedom Awards," Zenger's Newsmagazine, September 2, 2009, http://zengersmag.blog-spot.com/2009/09/presidents-former-advisor-attacks-him.html.

31 Jason Horowitz, "Democratic Operative Steve Hildebrand Goes Rogue," *The Washington Post*, April 1, 2010, http://www.washingtonpost.com/wp-dyn/content/article/2010/03/31/AR2010033103675.html.

32 Marshall Ganz, "How Obama Lost His Voice, and How He Can Get It Back," *The Los Angeles Times*," November 3, 2010, http://articles.latimes.com/2010/nov/03/opinion/la-oe-1103-ganz-obama-20101103.

33 Joshua Levy, "One Million Strong for Obama?" techPresident.com, January 26, 2007, https://techpresident.com/content/one-million-strong-obama.

34 Fred Stutzman, "The New Influencers: Stephen Demaura," techPresident.com, April 11, 2007, http://techpresident.com/blog-entry/new-influencers-stephen-demaura.

35 Micah L. Sifry, "ParkRidge47 Mystery Solved by HuffPost," techPresident.com, March 21, 2007, http://techpresident.com/blog-entry/parkridge47-mystery-solved-huffpost.

36 Micah L. Sifry, " 'Dear Mr. Obama,' The GOP's First Viral Video?" tech-President.com, September 12, 2008, http://techpresident.com/news/6342/dear-mr-obama-gops-first-viral-video-updated.

37 Nancy Scola, "Anti-Telecom Immunity Group Tops MyBarackObama.com," techPresident.com, June 2, 2008, http://techpresident.com/blog-entry/anti-telecom-immunity-group-tops-mybarackobamacom.

38 Andrew Rasiej and Micah L. Sifry, "The Web: 2008's Winning Ticket," Politico, November 12, 2012, http://www.politico.com/news/stories/1108/15520.html.

39 Timothy Stenovec, "Obama's 'Horses and Bayonets' Comment Goes Viral," Huffington Post, October 23, 2012, http://www.huffingtonpost.com/2012/10/23/horses-and-bayonets-debate-obama-video_n_2004038.html.

40 Marlow Stern, "Mitt Romney's 'Binders Full of Women' Comment Sets Internet Ablaze," The Daily Beast, October 17, 2012, http://www.thedailybeast.com/

articles/2012/10/17/mitt-romney-s-binders-full-of-women-comment-sets-internet-ablaze.html. See also http://bindersfullofwomen.tumblr.com/.

41 Peter Hamby, "Did Twitter Kill the Boys on the Bus? Searching for a Better Way to Cover a Campaign," Shorenstein Center at Harvard University, September 2013, http://shorensteincenter.org/2013/08/d80-hamby.

42 John Sides and Lynn Vavreck, *The Gamble: Choice and Chance in the 2012 Presidential Election* (Princeton University Press, Princeton, New Jersey, 2013).

43 Nate Silver, "Sept. 27: The Impact of the '47 Percent,'" FiveThirtyEight, *The New York Times*, September 28, 2013, http://fivethirtyeight.blogs.nytimes.com/2012/09/28/sept-27-the-impact-of-the-47-percent. "Ninety percent of 'game-changing' gaffes are less important in retrospect than they seem in the moment," Silver writes.

44 YouTube Trends Team, "Videos Mentioning Obama or Romney Top 2 Billion Views," YouTube Trends Blog, August 27, 2012, http://youtube-trends.blogspot.com/2012/08/videos-mentioning-obama-or-romney-top-2.html.

45 Micah L. Sifry, "User-Generated Online Video Swamping Official Obama, Romney Content on YouTube," techPresident.com, August 27, 2012, http://techpresident.com/news/22777/user-generated-online-video-swamping-official-obama-romney-content-youtube.

46 Michael Scherer, "Inside the Secret World of the Data Crunchers Who Helped Obama Win," *Time*, November 7, 2012, http://swampland.time.com/2012/11/07/inside-the-secret-world-of-quants-and-data-crunchers-who-helped-obama-win.

47 Author interview with a source involved in the Obama campaign's modeling program who asked to remain anonymous.

48 Author interview with Amelia Showalter, November 2012.

49 Micah L. Sifry, "Yes They Can: What Voters Have Lost and Campaigns Have Gained from 2008 to 2012," techPresident.com, March 13, 2012, http://techpresident.com/news/21902/yes-they-can-what-voters-have-lost-and-campaigns-have-gained-2008-2012.

50 Nick Judd, "How Obama for America Made Its Facebook Friends Into Effective Advocates," techPresident.com, November 19, 2012, http://techpresident.com/news/23159/how-obama-america-made-its-facebook-friends-effective-advocates.

51 Michael Scherer, op cit.

52 Dave Weigel, "'The Socially Awkward Do It Better,'" Slate, December 3, 2012, http://www.slate.com/articles/news_and_politics/politics/2012/12/rootscamp_meet_the_hip_geeks_who_beat_mitt_romney_and_helped_barack_obama.single.html.

53 Zeynep Tufekci, "Beware the Smart Campaign," *The New York Times*, November 16, 2012, http://www.nytimes.com/2012/11/17/opinion/beware-the-big-data-campaign.html.

54 Ethan Roeder, "I Am Not Big Brother," *The New York Times*, December 5, 2012, http://www.nytimes.com/2012/12/06/opinion/i-am-not-big-brother.html.

55 Author's recording.

56 Author's recording.

57 Robert M. Bond, et.al, "A 61-million-person experiment in social influence and political mobilization," *Nature* 489, pp 295–298, September 13, 2012, http://www.nature.com/nature/journal/v489/n7415/full/nature11421.html. (The full paper is available here http://fowler.ucsd.edu/massive_turnout.pdf.)

58 Ibid.

59 Micah L. Sifry and Joshua Levy, "Did Facebook Play Favorites with Obama?" techPresident.com, June 4, 2007, http://techpresident.com/blog-entry/did-facebook-play-favorites-obama.

60 Sarah Lai Stirland, "Facebook's Voting Reminder Message Isn't Working," techPresident.com, November 6, 2012, http://techpresident.com/news/23101/facebooks-voting-reminder-message-isnt-working.

61 Maeve Duggan and Joanna Brenner, "The Demographics of Social Media Users – 2012," Pew Internet & American Life Project, February 14, 2013; http://pewinternet.org/Reports/2013/Social-media-users/Social-Networking-Site-Users/Demo-portrait.aspx. While 67 percent of American Internet users are on Facebook, 72 percent of women and 62 percent of men are. 86 percent of *Internet* users aged 18–29 and 73 percent of internet users aged 30–49 are on it, compared to just 35 percent of people over 65. And 72 percent of urbanites are on it, compared to 63 percent of rural dwellers.

62 "Election 2012: President Exit Polls," *The New York Times*, http://elections.nytimes.com/2012/results/president/exit-polls.

63 Email communication with the author, November 15–19, 2013.

64 Author's recording.

65 Patrick Ruffini, "The GOP Talent Gap," *The Atlantic*, November 16, 2012, http://www.theatlantic.com/politics/archive/2012/11/the-gop-talent-gap/265333.

66 EngageDC, "Inside the Cave: An In-Depth Look at the Digital, Technology and Analytics Operations of Obama for America," December 2012, http://enga.ge/projects/inside-the-cave/.

67 David Drucker, "GOP Launches iPhone-Like, High-Tech Data Operation," Roll Call, May 1, 2013, http://blogs.rollcall.com/218/exclusive-gop-launches-data-modern-data-operation.

68 See http://rightonline.com/beta/agenda.

69 Author's recording.

70 Joseph Turow et al, "Americans Roundly Reject Tailored Political Advertising," University of Pennsylvania Annenberg School for Communication, July 24, 2012, http://www.asc.upenn.edu/news/Turow_Tailored_Political_Advertising.pdf.

71 See "DSPolitical, Home of the Political Cookie," YouTube.com, March 29, 2012, https://www.youtube.com/watch?v=lQ_Xa6FfyGQ.

72 Matthias Reynolds, "Targeted Victory Partners with Lotame to Expand Audience Targeting Platform," Targeted Victory blog, March 12, 2012, http://www.targetedvictory.com/2012/03/12/targeted-victory-partners-with-lotame-to-expand-audience-targeting-platform.

73 Micah L. Sifry, "Will Online Political Targeting Generate a Voter Backlash?" techPresident.com, August 7, 2012, http://techpresident.com/news/22688/will-online-political-targeting-generate-voter-backlash.

74 Peter Levine, "The New Manipulative Politics: Behaviorial Economics, Microtargeting, and the Choice Confronting Organizing for America," March 18, 2013, http://peterlevine.ws/?p=11049.

75 Author recording. The Google Political Innovation Summit was invitation-only and held under "Chatham House Rule," meaning that statements could be generally reported but not attributed directly to a named individual without their express permission.

76 Ibid.
77 Jake Coyle, "YouTube Says the Battle With TV is Over," Associated Press, May 2, 2013, http://tv.yahoo.com/news/youtube-says-battle-tv-already-over-040801343 .html.
78 Brian Fung, "Don't Be Surprised If Your TV Soon Seems To Knows Everything About Your Politics," *The Washington Post*, January 28, 2014, http://www.wash-ingtonpost.com/blogs/the-switch/wp/2014/01/28/dont-be-surprised-if-your-tv-soon-seems-to-know-everything-about-your-politics.

Big Email: The Politics of Passive Democratic Engagement

1 Interviews with the author, March 2010, cited in Micah L. Sifry, "How to Listen to Your Online Members: Debating the MoveOn Way," techPresident.com, March 26, 2010, http://techpresident.com/blog-entry/how-listen-your-online-members-debating-moveon-way.
2 Brian Christian, "The A/B Test: Inside the Technology That's Changing the Rules of Business," *Wired*, April 25, 2012, http://www.wired.com/business/2012/04/ff_abtesting. See also Dan Siroker, "How Obama Raised $60 Million By Running a Simple Experiment," Optimizely, November 29, 2010, http://blog.optimizely .com/2010/11/29/how-obama-raised-60-million-by-running-a-simple-experiment.
3 Kyle Rush, "Optimization at the Obama campaign: a/b testing," December 12, 2012, http://kylerush.net/blog/optimization-at-the-obama-campaign-ab-testing/.
4 See http://www.momsrising.org/page/moms/aboutmomsrising.
5 See http://boldprogressives.org/about.
6 See http://colorofchange.org/press/releases/2013/10/29/statement-rashad-robinson-sen-durbin-stand-your.
7 See https://secure.avaaz.org/en/ (total claimed as of December 17, 2013).
8 David Karpf, "Netroots Goes Global," *The Nation*, October 16, 2013, http:// www.thenation.com/article/176700/netroots-goes-global. It's worth noting that Brandzel got his start after activists in Australia and Germany respectively launched GetUp! and Campact, each aiming to emulate MoveOn's model. Brandzel visited GetUp! in Australia, realized it was making headway, and then convinced MoveOn to support his efforts to try to spread the model elsewhere. Most of these groups, including MoveOn, now collaborate on strategy and tacti-cal development through the Online Progressive Engagement Network. GetUp! co-founder Jeremy Heimans now runs Purpose.com, a for-profit consultancy that builds similar style campaigns and organizations for corporate and nonprofit clients.
9 Andy Kroll, "Powerful Tea Party Groups Internal Docs Leak—Read Them Here," *Mother Jones*, January 4, 2013, http://www.motherjones.com/politics/2012/12/ freedomworks-rich-donors-armey-kibbe-super-pac.
10 Patrick O'Connor, "Heritage Foundation Becomes a Handful for the GOP," *Wall Street Journal*, July 22, 2013, http://online.wsj.com/news/articles/SB10001424127 8873241443045786419640562831244.
11 David Karpf, *The MoveOn Effect: The Unexpected Transformation of American Political Advocacy* (New York, Oxford University Press, 2012), pp. 36–37.

12 Chris Nolan, "MoveOn.org: No Longer a Start-up or an Upstart,"
    PersonalDemocracy.com, December 22, 2004, http://personaldemocracy.com/
    content/moveonorg-no-longer-start-or-upstart.

13 Matt Bai, *The Argument: Billionaires, Bloggers, and the Battle to Remake
    Democratic Politics* (Penguin Group, New York, NY, 2007), pp. 67–91.

14 Zephyr Teachout, "Come Together, Right Now: The Internet's Unlit Fuse,"
    Personal Democracy Forum, November 17, 2004, http://personaldemocracy.
    com/feature/come-together-right-now-internets-unlit-fuse.

15 Interview with author, September 2013.

16 Ibid.

17 https://www.moveon.org/pac/news/1000bakesales.html.

18 Mark Jurkowitz, "Web Group Looks for Ad to Beat Bush," *The Boston Globe*,
    January 12, 2004, http://www.boston.com/news/politics/president/bush/
    articles/2004/01/12/web_group_looks_for_ad_to_beat_bush.

19 Lenore Palladino, Special MoveOn Council Update, December 28, 2009, http://
    campaignerworld.wordpress.com/2009/12/28/special-moveon-council-update/.

20 Bruce Bimber, Andrew Flanigan and Cynthia Stohl, *Collective Action in
    Organizations,* (Cambridge, 2012, Cambridge University Press), p, 115.

21 Ibid., pp-115–116.

22 See http://www.scribd.com/doc/165440031/PCCC-Syria-Memo-to-US-Congress.

23 See https://civic.moveon.org/Syriasurvey_support_or_oppose.html.

24 Email communication with author, September 4, 2013.

25 Anna Galland, "Syria Votes Are In. Here Are Our Next Steps," MoveOn.org email,
    September 4, 2013.

26 Micah White, "Clicktivism is ruining leftist activism," *The Guardian*, August 12,
    2010, http://www.theguardian.com/commentisfree/2010/aug/12/clicktivism-
    ruining-leftist-activism.

27 Beth Kanter, "How Many Free Agents Does it Take to Change A Nonprofit
    Fortress," Beth's Blog, June 4, 2010, http://www.bethkanter.org/lightbulb-
    fortress-freeagent.

28 http://www.reddit.com/r/politics/comments/e2to6/you_know_what_fuck_this_
    idea_that_we_cant_get.

29 Nick Judd, "'I Lose Sleep Over Upvotes – Seriously': How a Subreddit Became a
    Social Action," techPresident.com, December 14, 2010, http://techpresident.com/
    blog-entry/i-lose-sleep-over-upvotes-seriously-how-subreddit-became-social-
    action and Brian Ries, "Reddit Gets Political," The Daily Beast, November 9, 2010,
    http://www.thedailybeast.com/articles/2010/11/09/reddit-goes-political-net-
    neutrality-spurs-launch-of-redditpac.html.

30 See http://www.change.org/about/impact.

31 Micah L. Sifry, "Online Organizing 2.0: How Change.org Found Its Groove (and
    Moved to the Center of Online Politics)," techPresident, May 15, 2012, https://
    techpresident.com/news/22189/online-organizing-20-how-changeorg-found-its-
    groove-and-moved-center-online-politics.

32 *The Daily Show With Jon Stewart*, April 23, 2012, http://www.thedailyshow.com/
    watch/mon-april-23-2012/ben-rattray.

33 See https://www.change.org/petitions/let-girls-play-football-stop-the-
    discrimination-by-the-archdiocese-of-philadelphia-cyo-office.

34 See https://www.change.org/petitions/equinox-take-down-the-offensive-and-sexist-billboard-at-your-bethesda-gym.

35 See Seth Godin, "Flipping the Funnel," January 26, 2006, http://sethgodin.type-pad.com/seths_blog/2006/01/flipping_the_fu.html.

36 Sifry, op.cit., "Online Organizing 2.0 . . ."

37 Justin Ruben, "A Once-in-a-Generation Opportunity, and a Bottom-Up Revolution at MoveOn.org," December 3, 2012, http://www.huffingtonpost.com/justin-ruben/a-oncein-a-generation-opp_b_2233527.html.

38 Transcript from "Reinvent Real-Time Movements," Reinventors.net, November 6, 2013, http://reinventors.net/roundtables/reinvent-movements.

39 See http://campaigns.gofossilfree.org/petition/new.

40 See http://www.credomobilize.com/petition/new.

41 See http://youpower.democracyforamerica.com.

42 See http://www.coworker.org/petition/new.

43 Author notes from panel discussion at RootsCamp 2013, December 13, 2013.

44 Ibid.

45 Ibid.

46 See http://pac.petitions.moveon.org/sign/support-the-student-loan.

47 Micah L. Sifry, "In Defense of Change at Change.org," techPresident.com, October 25, 2012, https://techpresident.com/news/23047/defense-change-changeorg.

48 David Karpf, "Change.org and the Dilemmas of Success," techPresident.com, June 19, 2012, http://techpresident.com/news/22396/op-ed-changeorg-and-dilemmas-success.

49 See http://aaronkrager.com/wp-content/uploads/2012/10/Rebrand-InternalFAQs-Change.pdf.

50 "How Capitol Hill is Coping With the Surge in Citizen Advocacy," Congressional Management Foundation, 2005, http://www.congressfoundation.org/projects/communicating-with-congress/how-capitol-hill-is-coping-with-the-surge-in-citizen-advocacy.

51 "Communicating with Congress: How Citizen Advocacy is changing Mail Operations on Capitol Hill," Congressional Management Foundation, 2011, http://www.congressfoundation.org/storage/documents/CMF_Pubs/cwc-mail-operations.pdf.

52 Shayna Englin and Stefan Hankin, "The Advocacy Gap," November 1, 2012, http://englin.net/englin2013/wp-content/uploads/2012/11/AdvocacyGap-ResearchReport.pdf.

53 Clay Shirky, "Rethinking Representation," Personal Democracy Forum 2010, June 11, 2012, https://www.youtube.com/watch?v=P2GyPniW2eM.

54 Jake Brewer, "The Tragedy of Political Advocacy," The Huffington Post, October 25, 2010, http://www.huffingtonpost.com/jake-brewer/the-tragedy-of-political_b_773734.html.

55 See http://live.huffingtonpost.com/r/archive/segment/man-sentenced-for-public-sex-with-pool-toy/527d551bfe34447c8f000123.

56 See http://www.buzzfeed.com/erinchack/times-the-spongebob-writers-said-screw-logic.

57 Upworthy Insider, "What Actually Makes Things Go Viral Will Blow Your Mind. (Hint: It's Not Headlines Like This.)," December 5, 2013, http://blog.upworthy.com/post/69093440334/what-actually-makes-things-go-viral-will-blow-your.

58 Eliza Brooke," Video Site Upworthy Closes $8M Round, Will Build Revenue Through Sponsored Content," TechCrunch.com, Spetember 16, 2013, http://techcrunch.com/2013/09/16/meaningful-video-site-upworthy-closes-8m-will-build-revenue-through-sponsored-content.

59 Shirky, "Rethinking Representation," op. cit.

60 "What Actually Makes Things Go Viral Will Blow Your Mind. (Hint: It's Not Headlines Like This.)," December 5, 2013, http://blog.upworthy.com/post/69093440334/what-actually-makes-things-go-viral-will-blow-your.

61 See https://www.change.org/about/impact (accessed December 18, 2013, includes international members).

62 See https://secure.avaaz.org/en/ (accessed December 18, 2013, includes international members).

63 Byron Tau, "President Obama's data a powerful tool for Democrats," Politico.com, July 9, 2013, http://www.politico.com/story/2013/07/2014-elections-president-obama-email-list-93871.html.

64 See http://www.care2.com (accessed December 18, 2013).

65 Nick Berning, "MoveOn's 8 Million Members Vote Overwhelmingly to Oppose Military Action in Syria," September 4, 2013, http://front.moveon.org/moveons-8-million-members-vote-overwhelmingly-to-oppose-military-action-in-syria.

66 See http://credoaction.com/about/ (accessed December 18, 2013).

67 See http://sumofus.org/ (accessed December 18, 2013, includes international members)

68 See http://www.momsrising.org/page/moms/aboutmomsrising (accessed December 18, 2013).

69 See http://boldprogressives.org/about (accessed December 18, 2013).

70 See http://colorofchange.org/press/releases/2013/10/29/statement-rashad-robinson-sen-durbin-stand-your.

71 A. Trevor Thrall, et. al., "May We Have Your Attention Please? Human Rights NGOs and the Problem of Global Communication," *The International Journal of Press/Politics*, January 26, 2014.

The Way We Look to Us All

1 Author notes from IdealistNYC event, September 16, 2011. The goal of this event was to kick off a major new local organizing project in New York City, centered on recruiting "connectors" who would fan out across the city doing local community listening and organizing, building lateral neighbor-to-neighbor networks. The Occupy Wall Street protest in Zuccotti Park began the next week, subsuming the IdealistNYC effort.

2 Dave Parry, "It's Not the Public Internet, It's the Internet Public," Profound Heteregeneity, February 4, 2011, http://profoundheterogeneity.com/2011/02/its-not-the-public-internet-it-is-the-internet-public.

3 Sue Gardner, "The War for the Free and Open Internet – And How We Are Losing It," June 26, 2013, http://suegardner.org/2013/06/26/the-war-for-the-free-and-open-internet-and-how-we-are-losing-it.

4 See https://en.wikipedia.org/wiki/Special:Contributions/Sue_Gardner.

5 Dean Terry, "Enemy Graph Facebook Application," February 12, 2012, http://www.deanterry.com/post/18034665418/enemygraph.

6 See https://twitter.com/chrismessina/status/223115412.

7 Chris Messina, "Groups for Twitter; or A Proposal for Twitter Tag Channels," August 25, 2007, http://factoryjoe.com/blog/2007/08/25/groups-for-twitter-or-a-proposal-for-twitter-tag-channels.

8 Chris Messina, "Twitter Hashtags for Emergency Coordination and Disaster Relief," October 22, 2007, http://factoryjoe.com/blog/2007/10/22/twitter-hashtags-for-emergency-coordination-and-disaster-relief.

9 Chris Messina, "Why Didn't the Creator of Hashtag Patent the Idea?" http://www.quora.com/Hashtags/Why-didnt-the-creator-of-Hashtag-patent-the-concept.

10 Micah L. Sifry, "Split by SouthWest: My SXSW 2012 Diary," techPresident.com, March 15, 2012, http://techpresident.com/news/21922/split-southwest-my-sxsw-2012-diary.

11 "Why Indie Web," http://indiewebcamp.com/why.

12 Jeff Jarvis, "#f*ckyouwashington: The Story of a Hashtag and a Movement," The Huffington Post, August 24, 2011, http://www.huffingtonpost.com/jeff-jarvis/anti-washington-sentiment-_b_908117.html.

13 Matt Kruse, "Beware: Your Business Is At The Mercy Of Facebook! Social Fixer Page Deleted Without Explanation . . .," Social Fixer, September 12, 2013, http://socialfixer.com/blog/2013/09/12/beware-your-business-is-at-the-mercy-of-facebook-social-fixer-page-deleted-without-explanation.

14 Wael Ghonim, *Revolution 2.0: The Power of the People is Greater Than the People in Power* (Houghton Mifflin Harcourt, New York, NY 2012).

15 Nick Summers, "Google Will Remove All Blogger Sites That Monetize Adult Content, From June 30," The Next Web, http://thenextweb.com/google/2013/06/27/google-will-take-down-blogger-sites-on-june-30-which-host-adult-content-and-show-ads-for-adult-sites/.

16 Oliver Hotham, "The Sordid Tale of How I Was Censored by Straight Pride UK," August 11, 2013, https://oliverhotham.wordpress.com/2013/08/11/the-sordid-tale-of-how-i-was-censored-by-straight-pride-uk.

17 danah boyd, "Tumblr Disappeared Me," April 27, 2011, http://www.zephoria.org/thoughts/archives/2011/04/27/tumblr-disappeared-me.html.

18 Amy Wilentz, "Google Killed Me," February 13, 2013, http://amywilentz.tumblr.com/post/44228865923/google-killed-me.

19 Andy Baio, "YouTube's Content ID Disputes are Judged by the Accuser," March 2, 2012, http://waxy.org/2012/03/youtube_bypasses_the_dmca.

20 Alexis Madrigal, "Why You Should Want to Pay For Software, Instagram Edition," *The Atlantic*, December 17, 2012, http://www.theatlantic.com/technology/archive/2012/12/why-you-should-want-to-pay-for-software-instagram-edition/266367.

21 Mitch Kapor, "Architecture is Politics (and Politics is Architecture)," Mitch Kapor's Blog, April 22, 2006, http://blog.kapor.com/index9cd7.html?p=29.

22 Lawrence Lessig, *Code and Other Laws of Cyberspace* (Basic Books, NY, 2000).

23 Gardner, op. cit.

24 Gardner, op. cit.

25 Micah L. Sifry, "Gov 2.0 Summit: Tom Steinberg on .Gov Sites as Public Goods," techPresident.com, September 9, 2009, http://techpresident.com/blog-entry/gov-20-summit-tom-steinberg-gov-sites-public-goods.

26 Paul Simon and Forere Mothoeloa, "The Boy in the Bubble," *Graceland*, 1986.

27 I'm indebted to Oscar Salazar of Citivox for this notion.

28 See https://en.wikipedia.org/wiki/Wikipedia:SOPA_initiative.

29 William Harless, "Ben Berkowitz's Formula: Spot a Problem, Map It, Fix It," PBS Newshour, January 11, 2013, http://www.pbs.org/newshour/rundown/2013/01/ben-berkowitz.html.

30 Phone interview with author, November 26, 2013.

31 Interview with author at SeeClickFix headquarters in New Haven, November 22, 2013.

32 Ben Berkowitz, "Here Comes the Civic Boom," Ahoy Neighbor, March 2, 2013, http://benjaminberkowitz.blogspot.com/2013/03/here-comes-civic-boom.html.

33 MableX, "Other – city responsibility," SeeClickFix, August 29, 2013, http://seeclickfix.com/issues/714449-other-city-responsibility.

34 Phone interview with author, November 26, 2013.

35 Interview with author, November 22, 2013.

36 Ben Berkowitz, "A thank you to neighbors that keep me motivated to do better . . .," Ahoy Neighbor, September 12, 2013, http://benjaminberkowitz.blogspot.com/2013/09/a-thank-you-to-neighbors-that-keep-me.html.

37 Email to author, November 20, 2013.

38 Interview with author, November 22, 2013.

39 See http://www.seeclickfix.com/watch_area/296.

40 Interview with author, November 22, 2013.

41 Doug Hausladen, "Bring Back a Full-Service Supermarket to New Haven," SeeClickFix, March 10, 2010, http://seeclickfix.com/issues/25302-bring-back-a-full-service-supermarket-to-new-haven.

42 Interview with author, November 22, 2013.

43 "280 YMB Volkswagen Jetta just broken into by short man in broad daylight," SeeClickFix, November 17, 2013, http://seeclickfix.com/issues/824800.

44 See: http://forums.e-democracy.org/r/topic/3Pb7jbW5iTLKvNWoPFGAU7.

45 Facebook chat with author, November 18, 2013.

46 Bill McKibben, "Neighbors and Online Networks: Local Networks Are Bringing People Together in Vermont," *Yankee Magazine*, March 1, 2010.

47 Jamie Smith Hopkins, "Websites Aim to Make Neighborhoods More Neighborly: Online Options Multiply For Local Discussions, Connections," *The Baltimore Sun*, April 23, 2012, http://www.baltimoresun.com/business/bs-bz-nextdoor-neighborhood-sites-20120423,0,5169468.story.

48 Neal P. Goswami, "Front Porch Forum Now Statewide Across Vermont," *Barre Montpelier Times Argus* and *Rutland Herald*, September 11, 2013.

49 Heather Kelly, "NBC News Shuts Down Hyperlocal Site EveryBlock," CNN .com, February 7, 2013, http://www.cnn.com/2013/02/07/tech/innovation/

everyblock-closed. Sadly, the more than 600 comments on the NBC blog post, "Farewell, Neighbors," (February 7, 2013, http://blog.everyblock.com/2013/02/07/goodbye) announcing Everyblock's closure have been deleted.

50 Colleen Taylor, "Nextdoor Closes $21.6 Million in New Series B Funding To Take Its Neighborhood-Focused Social Network Global," TechCrunch.com, February 12, 2013, http://techcrunch.com/2013/02/12/nextdoor-closes-21-6-million-in-new-series-b-funding-to-take-its-neighborhood-focused-social-network-global.

51 Theda Skocpol, *Diminished Democracy: From Membership to Management in American Civic Life* (University of Oklahoma Press, Norman 2003), table 4.1, pp. 130–131.

52 Ibid., p. 105.

53 Author notes, public talk at Demos, New York City, April 2, 2004.

54 Skocpol, op. cit., p. 210.

55 Stephen D. Crocker, "How the Internet Got Its Rules," *The New York Times*, April 6, 2009, http://www.nytimes.com/2009/04/07/opinion/07crocker.html.

56 Ori Brafman and Rod Beckstrom, *The Starfish and the Spider* (The Penguin Group, New York, NY 2006), pp. 32–34.

57 Arthur Brisbane, "Who is Occupy Wall Street?" *The New York Times*, November 12, 2011, http://www.nytimes.com/2011/11/13/opinion/sunday/who-is-occupy-wall-street.html.

58 Marina Sitrin, *Horizontalism: Voices of Popular Power in Argentina* (AK Press, 2006).

59 Darcy K. Leach, "Culture and the Structure of Tyrannylessness," *The Sociological Quarterly* S4 (2013), pp. 183.

60 Interview with author, January 22, 2013.

61 Email communication with author, February 13, 2013.

62 Facebook chat with author, November 18, 2013.

63 Email communication with author, February 13, 2013.

64 Micah L. Sifry, "Can Social Software Change the World? Loomio Just Might," techPresident.com, February 18, 2013, http://techpresident.com/news/wegov/23517/can-social-software-change-world-loomio-just-might; and interview with Benjamin Knight, December 2, 2013.

65 David Meyer, "How the German Pirate Party's 'Liquid Democracy' Works," techPresident.com, May 7, 2012, http://techpresident.com/news/wegov/22154/how-german-pirate-partys-liquid-democracy-works.

66 Aaron Muszalski, "Shark Week 2012: How to Drive the Shark Conversation (Without Jumping It)", Upwell blog, August 7, 2012, http://www.upwell.us/shark-week-2012-how-drive-shark-conversation-without-jumping-it.

67 Ray Dearborn, "Shark Week's Over, But the Fun Has Just Started," Upwell blog, August 20, 2012, http://www.upwell.us/shark-weeks-over-fun-has-just-started.

68 Micah L. Sifry, "Using 'Big Listening' and 'Distributed Campaigning,' Upwell Seeks a Sea-Change in Ocean Organizing," techPresident.com, September 25, 2012, https://techpresident.com/news/22905/using-big-listening-and-distributed-campaigning-upwell-seeks-sea-change-ocean-organizing.

69 Greg Ray, "The Ocean is Broken," *Newcastle Herald*, October 18, 2013, http://www.theherald.com.au/story/1848433/the-ocean-is-broken.

70 Ray Dearborn, "Why Did 'The Ocean Is Broken' Go Viral?" Upwell blog, November 13, 2013, http://www.upwell.us/why-did-ocean-broken-go-viral.

71 Aaron Muszalski, "Ocean Acidification vs The Kardashians, Part Deux: The Gulf is Even Wider Online," Upwell blog, July 9, 2012, http://www.upwell.us/ocean-acidification-vs-kardashians-part-deux-gulf-even-wider-online.

72 Alistair Croll, "Big Data is Our Generation's Civil Rights Issue, And We Don't Know It," http://solveforinteresting.com/big-data-is-our-generations-civil-rights-issue-and-we-dont-know-it.

73 Spatial Information Design Lab, "Justice Reinvestment New Orleans," February 2009, http://www.spatialinformationdesignlab.org/MEDIA/JR_NewOrleans.pdf.

74 Justice Reinvestment Initiative, Vera Institute of Justice, http://www.vera.org/project/justice-reinvestment-initiative?qt-projects_justice_reinvestment_in=9#qt-projects_justice_reinvestment_in.

Coda: The Trouble We Face; The Opportunity We Have

1 Glenn Greenwald, "NSA Collecting Phone Records of Millions of Verizon Customers Daily," *The Guardian*, June 5, 2013, http://www.theguardian.com/world/2013/jun/06/nsa-phone-records-verizon-court-order.

2 Barton Gellman and Laura Poitras, "U.S., British Intelligence Mining Data From Nine U.S. Internet Companies in Broad Secret Program," *The Washington Post*, June 6, 2013, http://www.washingtonpost.com/investigations/us-intelligence-mining-data-from-nine-us-internet-companies-in-broad-secret-program/2013/06/06/3a0c0da8-cebf-11e2-8845-d970ccb04497_story.html; Glenn Greenwald and Ewen MacAskill, "NSA Prism Program Taps In To User Data of Apple, Google and Others," *The Guardian*, June 6, 2013, http://www.theguardian.com/world/2013/jun/06/us-tech-giants-nsa-data.

3 Glenn Greenwald and Laura Poitras, "Edward Snowden: The Whistleblower Behind the NSA Surveillance Revelations," *The Guardian*, June 9, 2013, http://www.theguardian.com/world/2013/jun/09/edward-snowden-nsa-whistleblower-surveillance.

4 See the Electronic Frontier Foundation's "Timeline of NSA Domestic Spying" for a complete set of sources for these facts: https://www.eff.org/nsa-spying/timeline; Julian Sanchez, "Decoding the Summer of Snowden," CATO Policy Report, November/December 2013, http://www.cato.org/policy-report/novemberdecember-2013/decoding-summer-snowden, and Barton Gellman and Ashkan Soltani, "NSA Surveillance Program Reaches "Into the Past" to Retrieve, Replay Phone Calls," *The Washington Post*, March 18, 2014, http://www.washingtonpost.com/world/national-security/nsa-surveillance-program-reaches-into-the-past-to-retrieve-replay-phone-calls/2014/03/18/226d2646-ade9-11e3-a49e-76adc9210f19_story.html

5 Leonard Downie Jr., "The Obama Administration and the Press," Committee to Protect Journalists, October 10, 2013, https://www.cpj.org/reports/2013/10/obama-and-the-press-us-leaks-surveillance-post-911.php.

6 Marisa Taylor and Jonathan S. Landay, "Obama's Crackdown Views Leaks as Aiding Enemies of U.S.," McLatchy Washington Bureau, June 20, 2013, http://www.mcclatchydc.com/2013/06/20/194513/obamas-crackdown-views-leaks-as.html.

7   Jonathan Weisman, "House Defeats Effort to Rein In N.S.A. Data Gathering," *The New York Times*, July 24, 2013, http://www.nytimes.com/2013/07/25/us/politics/house-defeats-effort-to-rein-in-nsa-data-gathering.html.

8   Ariel Edwards-Levy and Sunny Freeman, "Americans Still Can't Decide Whether Edward Snowden Is A 'Traitor' Or A 'Hero,' Poll Finds," Huffington Post, October 30, 2013, http://www.huffingtonpost.com/2013/10/30/edward-snowden-poll_n_4175089.html.

9   *Klayman v Obama*, United States District Court for the District of Columbia, Civil Action No. 12-0851 (RJL), December, 16, 2013, https://www.document-cloud.org/documents/900428-obamansa.html.

10 John Cassidy, "Snowden's Solution: More Encryption, Better Watchdogs," *The New Yorker*, March 10, 2014, http://www.newyorker.com/online/blogs/johncassidy/2014/03/snowdens-solution-more-encryption-and-better-watchdogs.html.

11 Bruce Schneier, "The Battle for Power on the Internet," *The Atlantic*, October 24, 2013, http://www.theatlantic.com/technology/archive/2013/10/the-battle-for-power-on-the-internet/280824/.

OR Books

PUBLISHING THE POLITICS OF THE INTERNET

WikiLeaks and the Age of Transparency
MICAH L. SIFRY

Cypherpunks: Freedom and the Future of the Internet
JULIAN ASSANGE WITH JACOB APPELBAUM, ANDY MÜLLER-
MAGUHN, AND JÉRÉMIE ZIMMERMANN

Hacking Politics: How Geeks, Progressives, the Tea Party,
Gamers, Anarchists and Suits Teamed Up to Defeat SOPA and
Save the Internet
DAVID MOON, PATRICK RUFFINI, AND DAVID SEGAL (EDITORS)

When Google Met WikiLeaks
JULIAN ASSANGE

Program or Be Programmed: Ten Commands for a Digital Age
DOUGLAS RUSHKOFF

Technocreep: The Surrender of Privacy and the Capitalization
of Intimacy
THOMAS P. KEENAN

Tweets From Tahrir: Egypt's Revolution as It Unfolded, in the
Words of the People Who Made It
NADIA IDLE AND ALEX NUNNS (EDITORS)

The Passion of Bradley Manning: The Story of the Suspect
Behind the Largest Security Breach in U.S. History
CHASE MADAR

Freeloading: How Our Insatiable Appetite for Free Content
Starves Creativity
CHRIS RUEN

For more information, visit our
website at www.orbooks.com